RISING SUN OVER BORNEO

Rising Sun over Borneo

The Japanese Occupation of Sarawak, 1941–1945

Ooi Keat Gin

Lecturer
School of Humanities
Universiti Sains Malaysia
Malaysia

First published in Great Britain 1999 by
MACMILLAN PRESS LTD
Houndmills, Basingstoke, Hampshire RG21 6XS and London
Companies and representatives throughout the world

A catalogue record for this book is available from the British Library.

ISBN 0-333-71260-9

First published in the United States of America 1999 by
ST. MARTIN'S PRESS, INC.,
Scholarly and Reference Division,
175 Fifth Avenue, New York, N.Y. 10010

ISBN 0-312-21714-5

Library of Congress Cataloging-in-Publication Data
Ooi, Keat Gin, 1959–
Rising sun over Borneo : the Japanese occupation of Sarawak,
1941–1945 / Ooi Keat Gin.
p. cm.
Includes bibliographical references and index.
ISBN 0-312-21714-5 (cloth)
1. Sarawak—History—Japanese occupation, 1941–1945. I. Title.
DS598.37.O65 1998
940.53'5954—dc21   98–38442
                                                        CIP

© Ooi Keat Gin 1999

This book is printed on paper suitable for recycling and made from fully managed and
sustained forest sources.

10   9   8   7   6   5   4   3   2   1
08   07   06   05   04   03   02   01   00   99

Printed and bound in Great Britain by
Antony Rowe Ltd, Chippenham, Wiltshire

For

Saw Ean and **Saw Lian**

who abhor politics and wars

Contents

List of Tables

List of Illustrations and Maps

Illustrations

Maps

Preface

One of the neglected periods in Sarawak historiography is the Japanese occupation of December 1941 to September 1945, which has received scant attention not only from local historians but also from foreign scholars. My research and interest on the Brooke era and the Crown Colony period has brought my attention to this lacuna in the historiography of Sarawak. The importance of this albeit brief period is undoubted but, curiously, it has attracted few scholastic endeavours, unlike other epochs.

My preoccupation with government policies and their impact on multi-ethnic society has encouraged me to pursue research into the occupation period. This present study focuses on Japanese wartime policies and their implementation, and the consequent effects these policies had on the local population. Each ethnic group (including the European community) is examined to evaluate their reactions and responses to the Japanese military government, and its policies towards them. The effects of the Japanese period on post-war developments will gauge and evaluate the significance and influence of this short domination by a non-Western power and the extent to which the changes, if any, were or were not beneficial to the country.

Furthermore, apart from filling this lacuna in Sarawak historiography, the primary objective of this study is to determine to what extent the Japanese occupation of three years and eight months was a major watershed in Sarawak's historical development. Specifically it is intended to consider whether the Japanese occupation initiated developments that transformed Sarawak's history (in effect, whether the occupation can be seen as a turning point); or alternatively, whether the years of the occupation were no more than a rude interruption in the country's historical development without any significant or lasting impact either physically on the land or mentally in the hearts and minds of the populace.

If not for the generous support afforded by the Centre for South-East Asian Studies at the University of Hull for the years 1994–95, for internal travel within the United Kingdom, the preliminary draft and notes of this study would still remain in one of my boxes at home. I am most grateful for the assistance rendered by Professor V. T. King, the then Director of the Centre. The financial kick-start to this venture, however, is owed to two Universiti Sains Malaysia Short-Term Research Grants which funded the research of certain sections of this study. In this connection, I must thank my colleague, Associate Professor Abdul Rahman Ismail, for his 'unique helping hand' in securing one of the research grants. I owe a debt of gratitude to The Toyota Foundation for their generous funding for archival research in London, Oxford and Canberra. I wish to thank Ms Yumiko Himemoto-Hiraishi, the Foundation's programme officer, for her assistance and support.

Interest in this topic of study dates back to 1983 when collection of some materials begun. I wish to thank Mr Loh Chee Ying, former archivist of the Sarawak Museum and State Archives, for 'uncovering' some materials relating to the Japanese period. Likewise, to my friend in Kuching, Fabian Liaw King Nyen, I owe a debt of thanks for his help. To Dr Yuen Choy Leng, formerly of Universiti Sains, Malaysia, go my thanks for introducing me to things Japanese, and at the same time encouraging me to focus my research interest on East Malaysia.

Some preliminary proposals and initial ideas in this study were presented at the Symposium of the Japanese Occupation in South-East Asia, under the auspices of The Toyota Foundation, Tokyo, Japan, which was organized by the Department of History at the National University of Singapore from 13 to 17 December 1995. My paper entitled 'Japanese Attitudes towards the Indigenous Peoples of Sarawak, 1941–1945' was discussed then. I wish to thank my co-panellist,

Professor Hara Fujio (Institute of Developing Economies, Tokyo), Professor Cheah Boon Kheng (formerly of Universiti Sains Malaysia), Associate Professor E. Bruce Reynolds (San Jose State University, San Jose), Dr Elly Touwen-Bouwsma (Netherlands State Institute for War Documentation), and Dr Paul H. Kratoska (National University of Singapore), the symposium organizer.

Research for this study took me to archives in the United Kingdom, Australia and Sarawak. I wish to extend my appreciation to the archivists and their helpful staff at the Department of Documents, Imperial War Museum, London; the Public Record Office, Kew; Rhodes House Library, Oxford; National Archives of Australia and the Australian War Memorial Research Centre, Canberra; and the Sarawak Museum and State Archives, Kuching. For secondary source materials I relied on the Brynmor Jones Library, University of Hull; the University Library of the National University of Singapore; National Library of Australia and the Australian National University Libraries (Menzies, Chifley, Law), Canberra; and Perpustakaan Utama I, Universiti Sains, Malaysia, Penang. To the librarians and their staff, a big thank you for all your assistance. Special acknowledgement of gratitude is reserved for these individuals: Mrs Clare Brown and Mrs Amanda Hill, former and present archivists, respectively, of Rhodes House Library; Mr Nick Forbes, of the Public Record Office; Mr Roderick W. A. Suddaby, the Keeper of the Department of Documents, and Mrs Rosemary Tudge of the Department of Sound Records, Imperial War Museum; Dr Peter Stanley and Ian Smith of the Australian War Memorial Research Centre; the Reading Room staff of the National Archives of Australia; and Ms Wong Sook Jean, head of acquisitions, Perpustakaan Universiti Sains, Malaysia.

Professor R. H. W. Reece of Murdoch University, Perth, deserves my gratitude for the photographs reproduced herein. To Pauline Khng and Dr Tim Huxley, thanks for your kind and timely assistance and hospitality. My fruitful stay in Canberra was owed to Professor Anthony Reid and Professor

Hank Nelson, of the Division of Pacific and Asian History, Research School of Pacific and Asian Studies, Australian National University.

To Mr T. M. Farmiloe, Publishing Director of Macmillan Press, let me take this opportunity to thank you for your patience, confidence and faith in me. I wish also to thank those at St Martin's Press, New York, for co-publishing this work.

For Frauke Franckenstein: 'Through thick and thin at the archives.' Thanks for the helping hand. And in London, for the companionship.

In appreciation for his moral support, a token of appreciation is here reserved for my old friend, Teoh Boon Hoe.

To my mother, Madam Tan Ai Gek, who lived through the Japanese period in George Town, Penang, and my sisters, Saw Lian and Saw Ean, your love and understanding I treasure.

Tanjung Bungah   OOI KEAT GIN
Penang

List of Abbreviations

ADO	Assistant District Officer
AIF	Australian Imperial Force
ARP	Air Raid Precaution
AS	*Asian Survey*
AWMA	Australian War Memorial Archives, Canberra
BBCAU	British Borneo Civil Affairs Unit
BCL	Borneo Company Limited
BMA	British Military Administration
BNB	British North Borneo (Sabah)
BRB	*Borneo Research Bulletin*
CCP	Chinese Communist Party
CQ	*The China Quarterly*
DFS	Direction Finding Station
DO	District Officer
HIM	His Imperial Majesty
HMAS	His/Her Majesty's Australian Ship
HMSO	His/Her Majesty's Stationery Office
IA	*International Affairs*
IIL	India Independence League
IWM	Imperial War Museum, London
JAWM	*Journal of the Australian War Memorial*
JMBRAS	*Journal of the Malaysian Branch Royal Asiatic Society*
JMHSSB	*Journal of the Malaysian Historical Society (Sarawak Branch)*
JSEAS	*Journal of Southeast Asian Studies*
KMT	Kuomintang
MAS	*Modern Asian Studies*
MNU	Malay National Union
MPAJA	Malayan Peoples' Anti-Japanese Army
NCO	Non-commissioned officer
NSW	New South Wales, Australia
PA	*Pacific Affairs*

POWs	Prisoners of War
PRC	People's Republic of China
PRO	Public Record Office, Kew
RA	Royal Artillery
RAE	Royal Australian Engineers
RAAF	Royal Australian Air Force
RAF	Royal Air Force
RASC	Royal Australian Service Corp
RHL	Rhodes House Library, Oxford
SAR	*Sarawak Administration Report*
SARFOR	Sarawak Forces
SCA	Sarawak Chinese Association
SDA	Sarawak Dayak Association
SG	*Sarawak Gazette*
SGG	*Sarawak Government Gazette*
SMA	Sarawak Museum Archives, Kuching
SMJ	*Sarawak Museum Journal*
SRD	(Australian) Services Reconnaissance Department
ST	*Sarawak Tribune*
SUPP	Sarawak United People's Party
WO	War Office (Series)

Glossary

adat	customs, beliefs and traditional practices
bejalai	Iban customary embarkation of a long journey or wandering to seek one's fortune and fame
dan	and
datu	Malay chieftains
guncho	district officer
Gunseibu	Japanese term for military government
jikeidan	auxiliary vigilante corps
kampung	Malay village
Kapitan China	Brooke-appointed Chinese headman of a Chinese same-dialect community
Kempeitai	Japanese military police
ken-sanji	councillor; member of *Ken Sanjikai*
Ken Sanjikai	Prefectural Advisory District Council
Kuo-yu	vernacular Mandarin (Chinese) language
kyodotai	militia recruited from local inhabitants
lari	a verb, meaning 'to run'
Mem	a shortened version of 'Madam'; general term to address European women
Nampo	Japanese term denoting the 'Southern Area/Region': that is, the countries of South-East Asia; equivalent to the Chinese *Nanyang*, meaning the 'South Seas'
nipah	thatch-palm; *nipa fruticans*
Nippon-go	Japanese language
padi	rice plant; unhusked rice or rice in the ear; *Oryza sativa*
pangeran	honorific of Brunei nobles
Penghulu	a Brooke-created socio-political title denoting an Iban headman; a position of higher status than a *tuai rumah*

perabangan	the *abang* class; *abang* is the title of the sons of *datu*
semut	ant
simpan duit	save money
sook ching	Chinese term for symbolic cleansing; purification through deeds
-shu	prefecture/province
towkay	Chinese Hokkien dialect term of address of a head of a commercial enterprise, shopkeeper, entrepreneur; an honorific denoting respect for a person of wealth and influence
tuai rumah	headman of longhouse
Tuan	'Mr' or 'Sir'; a term of address for a person of authority; commonly used for European men
ubi-kayu	cassava-manioc; tapioca
VP-Day	Victory in the Pacific Day, 15 August 1945
zaibatsu	conglomerate of companies/business houses

Spelling, Usage of Terms and Currencies

In general, the spelling and names of places and of people are retained as they appear in documents. In the case of Japanese names, personal names precede the family name as adopted in most archival material. English orthography is preferred to Dutch, even for names and terms in Dutch Borneo. 'Dayak' or 'Dyak' are used interchangeably is applied to mean 'Sea Dayak' or 'Iban'. Where it is known, the different Chinese speech groups (Hokkien, Teochew, Hakka, and others) are designated.

The reference of administrative delineation of divisions – First, Second, Third, Fourth and Fifth – are in accordance to pre-war Brooke usage and not to the current boundaries.

Unless stated otherwise, all currencies refer to the Sarawak Dollar, which was tied to the Straits Settlements Dollar, and tended to fluctuate in value. From 1906 Straits Dollar was pegged to Sterling at the rate of $1 to 2s 4d, or $8.57 to £1. This rate was generally maintained until December 1941.

1 Sarawak and its Peoples

Sarawak lies in the north-western part of Borneo, sharing its borders to the north-east with Sabah (formerly British North Borneo), a fellow member state of the Federation of Malaysia, and the kingdom of Negeri Brunei Darrulsalam; and to the south-east and south-west with Indonesian Kalimantan (formerly Dutch Borneo). Sarawak is about 124 485 square kilometres (48 250 square miles) and constitutes nearly 38 per cent of the total area of Malaysia. Despite its large land area, its population in 1995 was only 1.9 million, compared to the total population of Malaysia of 20.7 million.[1]

Topographically Sarawak has three distinct units: an alluvial and swampy coastal plain, a wide belt of undulating hilly terrain, and a rugged and mountainous interior rising above 1200 metres (4000 feet). The rivers flowing south-east-north-west into the South China Sea form a myriad drainage network criss-crossing the country. Rivers and streams remained the natural highways and an important means of transport and communications, particularly in the inland regions. Three-quarters of Sarawak is still under dense tropical rainforest, with large areas still inaccessible.

The territorial borders of Sarawak when it was first granted to an English gentleman-adventurer, James Brooke, by Sultan Omar Ali Saifuddin II of Brunei in 1841, constituted the area from Lundu to the Sadong River. Subsequently Sarawak's political borders were relentlessly pushed eastwards at the expense of Brunei and these borders reached their present configuration by 1909.

Under Brooke rule, Sarawak was divided into five administrative units called 'Divisions', which were designated as First, Second, Third, Fourth and Fifth (see Map 1.1). Delineation was based on river basins: First (Lundu, Sarawak, Sadong, Samarahan); Second (Lupar, Saribas, Krian); Third (Rejang, Balleh, Balui); Fourth (Bintulu, Baram, Tinjar); and Fifth

1

Map 1.1   Relief, drainage and divisional boundaries of Sarawak before 1941

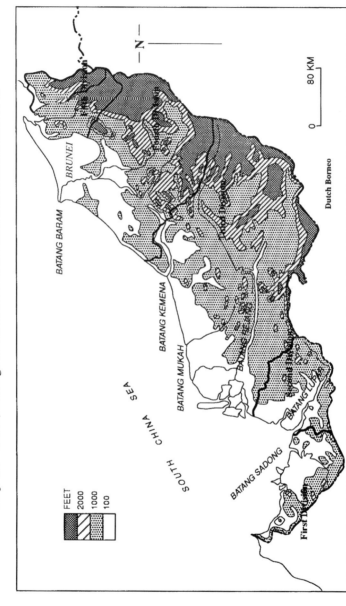

Source: After James C. Jackson, *Sarawak: A Geographical Survey of a Developing State* (London: University of London Press, 1968) p. 23.

(Lawas, Limbang Trusan). Each Division was sub-divided into districts. A Resident was in charge of a Division; the most senior was the Resident of the First Division who was next in authority to the Rajah himself. District Officers (DOs) and Assistant District Officers (ADOs), as their titles imply, administered a district and a sub-district respectively. All these administrative positions were held by Europeans; the majority of Brooke officers were recruited from Britain, and a few hailed from Europe. The DO and the ADO were assisted by a Native Officer, who was knowledgeable about local customs and traditions, and familiar with the people and terrain of the locality. The majority of these positions were held by upper-class Malays, the *perabangan* class, who were not only well versed in native *adat*, Muslim practices and traditional customs, but also, and more importantly, had the respect and trust of the local multi-racial inhabitants.

The increase in population was gradual and its spatial pattern had always been scattered and rural-based with a few urban centres of concentration, namely Kuching (the capital), Sibu (the chief port) and Miri (centre of the oil industry). Table 1.1 shows the population estimate of 1939 and the figures from the census of 1947.

THE INDIGENOUS INHABITANTS

Indigenous peoples as defined by 'Order No. I-1 (Interpretation) 1933' meant:

> a subject of His Highness the Rajah of any race which is now considered to be indigenous to the State of Sarawak as set out in the Schedule: Bukitans, Bisayahs, Dusuns, Dayaks (Sea), Dayaks (Land), Kadayans, Kayans, Kenyahs (including Sabups and Sipengs), Kajangs (including Sekapans, Kejamans, Lahanans, Punans, Tanjongs and Kanowits), Lugats, Lisums, Malays, Melanos, Muruts, Penans, Sians, Tagals, Tabus, [and] Ukits. And any admixture of the above with each other.[2]

4 *Rising Sun Over Borneo*

Table 1.1 Population of Sarawak in 1939 and 1947

Community	1939	%	1947	%
Iban (Sea Dayak)	167 700	34.2	190 326	34.8
Chinese	123 626	25.2	145 158	26.6
Malay	92 709	18.9	97 469	17.9
Land Dayak	36 963	7.5	42 195	7.7
Melanau	36 772	7.5	35 560	6.5
Other Indigenous*	27 532	5.6	29 867	5.5
Others+	4 579	0.9	5 119	0.9
European	704	0.2	691	0.1
Total	490 585	100.0	546 385	100.0

* Minorities such as Kayan, Kenyah, Kedayan, Murut, Bisayah, Punan, Kelabit, Orang Hulu, Dusun, and others.
+ Includes Javanese, Indian and Ceylonese/Sinhalese, Bugis, Filipino, Arabs, Bataks, Siamese and Banjorese.
Source: L. W. Jones, *Sarawak: Report on the Census of Population taken on 15th June 1960* (Kuching: Government Printing Office, 1962) p. 59.

The indigenous peoples accounted for about three-quarters of the country's total population during the inter-war years. Table 1.2 lists the principal indigenous groups and their population in 1939 and 1947; and Table 1.3 has the population figures of the other minor native communities in 1947.

Unlike in other European colonized territories, the term 'native', referring to Sarawak's indigenous inhabitants, was a term of endearment used by the Brooke administration, and it possessed none of the derogatory attributes of its usage that it had in Africa or the West Indies. On the contrary, being considered 'native' in Brooke Sarawak carried with it certain privileges not enjoyed by non-natives, principally Chinese. Brooke paternalism enacted legislation to shield native peoples from all forms of exploitation by both Chinese and Europeans, especially in matters relating to land acquisition and utilization. Certain native groups of the interior were even exempted from prosecution for debts.[3]

Table 1.2 Population of the principal indigenous groups, 1939 and 1947

Groups	1939	%	1947	%
Iban (Sea Dayak)	167 700	46	190 326	48
Malay	92 709	26	97 469	25
Land Dayak	36 963	10	42 195	11
Melanau	36 772	10	35 560	9
Others	27 532	8	29 867	7
Total	361 676	100	395 417	100

Source: L. W. Jones, *Sarawak: Report on the Census of Population taken on 15th June 1960* (Kuching: Government Printing Office, 1962) p. 50.

Table 1.3 Population of other minor indigenous groups, 1947

Community	Number
Kayan	6 183
Kenyah	5 507
Kedayan	5 334
Murut	3 290
Bisayah	2 058
Punan and Others	5 883
Total	28 255

Source: L. W. Jones, *Sarawak: Report on the Census of Population taken on 15th June 1960* (Kuching: Government Printing Office, 1962) p. 55.

Sarawak, the area covering the river basins of Samarahan and Sarawak, in the early nineteenth century, was a vassal domain of the Brunei sultanate which assigned its governance to local Malay chiefs, the *datu*. However, when antimony was discovered in the 1820s and a market was established with the opening of Singapore, a Brunei *pangeran* named Mahkota was assigned to oversee the production of this commodity. But dissatisfaction with Mahkota's rule prompted the Malays and Land Dayaks to launch the anti-Brunei revolt of 1836–40. The rebellion ended with the successful intervention of James Brooke to suppress the uprising in the sultanate's favour. For his feat, James was rewarded with the fiefdom of Sarawak; he was proclaimed the first white rajah on 1 August 1842. In line with his concept of indirect rule, James restored his former enemies, the Sarawak Malay *datu* – the *Patinggi*, the *Bandar* and the *Temanggong* – to their former political functions[4] and enlisted them into his government as native advisers with whom he consulted informally.[5] Members of the *datu* class, the Malay ruling elite, were recruited into the Brooke civil service as Native Officers with duties as assistants and advisers and consultants to European Residents and DOs. Malays also staffed the police force as constables under European officers and as schoolteachers serving in government Malay schools.

As members of the Brooke bureaucracy and police force, the Malays were fairly numerous in the urban areas. Pockets of Malay communities were found in the delta areas of the Batang Lupar and Rejang, and in the districts bordering Brunei. The economic activities of the rural Malay peasantry included wet-rice planting, mixed gardening, the growing of various tropical fruits, rubber and coconut cultivation, coastal fishing, boat-building and petty trading.

The Sea Dayaks or Ibans, the largest native group, were largely rural-based with concentrations in the Batang Lupar, Saribas and Rejang river systems. Although some practised wet-rice cultivation in the lower reaches of rivers and deltaic flatlands, the majority were shifting cultivators of hill rice in the hilly inland areas. Their economy was basically subsistence, but some cash crops, such as rubber, were cultivated, and they also collected jungle produce to supplement their normally meagre income. The Sarawak Rangers, Brooke's regular army, consisted largely of Iban recruits. Small numbers of Ibans also joined the police force.

Melanau settlements dotted the low-lying coastal plains converging on the lower reaches of the Igan, Oya, Mukah, Balingian, Tatau and Kemena rivers. The districts of Sarikei, Sibu, Bintulu, Binatang and Mukah were their strongholds.

Although sago cultivation and production had been the dominant economic activities since the early nineteenth century, Melanaus were also involved in the timber and fishing industry. The Land Dayaks were swidden agriculturalists of hill-rice and longhouse dwellers like the Ibans. Their concentrations were almost exclusively in the upper reaches of the Lundu, Sarawak, Kayan, Sadong and Samarahan rivers.

Kedayans, Muruts and Bisayahs practised wet-rice cultivation in the coastal and interior districts of the Trusan and Lawas rivers. Existing almost in isolation in the remote mountainous uplands of the headwaters of the Baram and the Bario highlands, the Kelabits were equally as adept as the Muruts in wet-rice planting. These wet-rice farmers utilized irrigation to overcome the problems of low or irregular rainfall.

Kayan and Kenyah longhouse settlements were scattered in the valleys of the Upper Rejang and Balui, the Baram basin, and the branches of the Ulu Kemena river. These two communities shared similar social and cultural traits. Both were primarily shifting cultivators of hill rice, although some also practised cash-cropping of rubber, coffee and groundnuts. Kajangs comprised a constellation of diverse groups: 'Kanowit Dayaks', Tanjongs, Punan Bas, Skapans, Kajamans and Lahanans. They inhabited the Upper Rejang valley, as far upstream as Belaga and beyond. Like the Ibans, they lived in longhouses, but linguistically and culturally their affinity was to the coastal Melanaus. However, in terms of economic activities and general lifestyle, they were more akin to their immediate neighbours, the Kenyahs and Kayans. The nomadic Penans were jungle dwellers scattered thinly in the deep forests between the Upper Rejang and the Baram basin. They subsisted as hunters and gatherers of forest produce.

Amicability pervades inter-ethnic relations among Brooke Sarawak's plural subjects. Although there were pockets of disaffection with the government in the upriver and interior districts,[6] the 1930s as a whole witnessed the cessation of inter-tribal warfare. Malay-Iban relations had always been on a stable and friendly footing; acknowledgement of the Malays as agents of the Brooke government by Ibans and other indigenous groups allowed the administration of the country with negligible difficulty. The long association of peaceful existence among the various native peoples with the immigrant Chinese, the largest non-indigenous group, fostered a sense of co-existence. The main interaction the Chinese had with indigenous peoples was in economic activities where mutual benefits dictated the relationship of the Chinese merchant entrepreneur and the native producer of commodities and consumer of manufactured goods.

Religious diversity was a hallmark of Sarawak's indigenous communities. While Malays and a section of the Melanau community embraced Islam, a considerable number of Ibans and some Melanaus were Christian converts. However, the large majority of native peoples maintained their animist beliefs and adhered to their *adat*. Notwithstanding such religious diversity, inter-religious problems were conspicuously absent. Muslims, Christians of various denominations and pagans lived side by side and interacted without rancour or trouble.

Educationally amongst the indigenous peoples, the Malays were the most advanced in terms of access to schools. Government Malay schools were established in the major towns to provide a basic education for the Malay upper and middle class from whence the Brooke civil service recruited. But, for the bulk of the Malay population of peasant farmers and fishermen residing in the rural areas, educational opportunities were minimal.[7] The Brooke government entrusted the education of the non-Malay indigenous peoples to Christian missionaries. The various Christian missions, in spite of managing a few major schools in Kuching, largely neglected their schools in the outstations which were few and understaffed. Like their Malay peasant counterparts, the majority of Ibans and other natives in the rural districts and upriver areas were barely touched by schools and education.[8]

Politically the native inhabitants were inert. Even the Malay elite harboured no political ambition. Unlike their counterparts in the Malay States, the Sarawak Malay middle class, comprising civil servants and schoolteachers, was inured to Indonesian anti-colonial struggles and few possessed socialist tendencies. The Malay community as a whole was content to support the Brooke Raj. The Ibans, too, did not demonstrate any political intentions. In fact, no native organized political movement existed.[9]

THE IMMIGRANT CHINESE

The Chinese, more than any other community in Brooke Sarawak, played a key role in economic development. The presence of a Chinese shophouse close to the government fort typified an outstation scene. From trading activities to cash-cropping, the Chinese played a major role in their advancement. Chinese economic success was shown by their domination of most branches of trade, in the cultivation of commercial crops, and as the bulk of the labour force in the extractive industries.

The utilitarian qualities of the Chinese extended to their contribution to the Brooke Treasury in the form of indirect taxation through government monopolies, namely those for opium and arrack, their recreational activities as compulsive gamblers, and their patronage of pawn shops. Furthermore, the Chinese were largely responsible for increasing customs duties through their trading activities and agricultural pursuits, coupled with their enormous appetite for imported rice and Western-manufactured goods.

Notwithstanding the accomplishments and contributions of the Chinese, the Brookes were suspicious of their intentions, and in general mistrustful of the whole community as a consequence of the events of 1857, when Chinese gold miners at Bau launched an attack on the Brooke government situated downriver at Kuching.[10] The episode was undoubtedly a great setback to the gold mining industry, but more importantly, the entire Chinese community in the country was blighted by the Brookes' fear of resistance that persisted throughout their rule. Apart from a few prominent Chinese community and business leaders, the Chinese population was treated with suspicion. As Chinese secret societies were blamed by

Brooke official circles for the events of 1857, such clandestine organizations were proscribed; those apprehended for involvement in (from the Brooke perspective) subversive organizations faced long terms of imprisonment, deportation or, for the leaders, even the death penalty.[11] Furthermore, the Brookes also resorted to precautionary measures by enforcing stricter immigration control, particularly during the 1920s and 1930s, when the political situation in mainland China became increasingly unstable. Tighter entry requirements and other arrangements (such as the 'guarantee system', whereby fellow clansmen or family members undertook to give an assurance of good behaviour on behalf of a newly arrived immigrant) were imposed to ensure that subversive elements, political agitators, and other malcontents fleeing the mainland did not enter Sarawak to disturb the relatively peaceful existence of the resident Chinese community. Immigration control was reinforced during the years of the Depression (1929–31) to alleviate the unemployment situation, but during the post-Depression period, strict control was maintained as one of the strategies to ensure the success of the Rubber Restriction Scheme.

The success of the implementation of strict immigration measures during the 1920s and 1930s was evidenced by the conspicuous absence of organized agitation by Leftist elements.[12] The Administration Report for 1934 proudly attested to Sarawak's immunity from the subversive activities that had plagued the Straits government, and boasted of the effectiveness of the strategies employed:

> Sedition is non-existent, and there was nowhere any unrest or political disturbance, the Chinese throughout the State remaining everywhere peaceful and law-abiding. There is no doubt that the State's freedom from political agitators and other undesirable characters is in a large measure due to the present strict control of immigration, and particularly to the good effects of the 'guarantee system,' which has now been operating satisfactorily for several years. It is, however, a fact that the Chinese in Sarawak show a noticeable lack of interest in politics in China.[13]

The status of the Chinese in the country remained ambiguous until 1931. The land laws of 1920 defined 'native' as a 'natural born subject of His Highness the Rajah', a category which included those Chinese born in the country as well as those who successfully acquired a certificate of naturalization.[14] In practice, however, the locally born Chinese were discriminated against and did not enjoy the same privileges accorded to Malays and other indigenous peoples particularly in relation to land matters. 'Native', then, was a term denoting nationality, and not ethnic status. However, the Land Rules of 1931 clearly excluded Chinese from the list of indigenes and the Land Rules of 1933 classified land according to whether it was in a 'Native Area' or 'Mixed Zone'. The Chinese as 'aliens' were prohibited from acquiring any rights to 'Native Area Land'. The growth in Chinese population during the 1920s and 1930s increased their demand for land. By 1939 the Chinese, who accounted for a quarter of the total population, had access to only one-tenth of the total land area in the country.[15]

Furthermore, within Brooke officialdom, the Chinese were seen as an immigrant community with transient tendencies. The fact that each year large numbers of Chinese voyaged back to the home country reinforced their transient image, even though most returned to Sarawak after a brief period. The notion of the Chinese coolie, who arrived penniless and after years of toil returned with his small savings to die in his native village, was largely unsubstantiated. No doubt some Chinese regarded Sarawak as a convenient place to seek a fortune, but few acquired it, and fewer still (for want of financial means and/or physical ability) retired to the homeland. Moreover, 'a considerable number of the wealthier and more powerful men in Kuching showed little inclination to leave their thriving businesses for retirement in China'.[16]

Besides this general perception of their transient status, their non-liability for capitation taxes, like the 'head' and 'door' taxes that the Malays, Ibans and other indigenous peoples were obliged to pay, placed the Chinese community in a different category from the rest. The payment of such taxes by the natives, apart from its financial aspect, had

socio-political connotations; it symbolized the close relationship between ruler and subjects, an expression of loyalty by
the latter to the former. The Chinese, then, were outside this
close affinal relationship. To carry this point further, with the
significant exception of the Chinese Court,[17] no Chinese
people were appointed to the administrative ranks of the
Brooke government or allowed to hold magisterial powers,[18]
although the English educated Chinese graduates of mission
schools were welcome to join the civil service in clerical
postions or the judiciary as court writers and interpreters.

Brooke-Chinese relations have been crudely summarized
in this manner:

> There had been no real attempts to understand the
> Chinese. Because of indirect rule most contacts with the
> Chinese had always been through a small group of privi-
> leged Chinese leaders who traditionally belonged to the
> wealthy and influential merchant class, or were appointed
> area headmen and *kapitans*, and through European and
> Asian members of the Sarawak civil service. The Rajahs
> had respected the Chinese for their industry but had also
> been suspicious of their activities and intentions, which no
> doubt arose out of mutual ignorance and common disdain
> for each other's way of life.[19]

Surprisingly, the Chinese community too, as a whole, also
expressed a general disinterest in politics. Although there
were adherents of the Kuomintang (KMT) and the Chinese
Communist Party (CCP) among Sarawak's Chinese, their
enthusiasm and involvement in political activities were nothing
compared to their compatriots in the Straits Settlements.
Anti-Japanese feelings among the Chinese were lukewarm
too; the campaign of boycotting Japanese goods was unim-
pressive.[20] The Singapore-based China Distress Relief Fund
had branches in Kuching and Sibu.

The outbreak of the Second Sino-Japanese War in 1937
rattled the characteristic Chinese nonchalance towards events
in the motherland. But even this momentous happening did
not stir the Chinese in Sarawak to a great display of patriotism

and anti-Japanese behaviour; their actions were limited to contributions to the China Relief Fund, the boycott of Japanese goods, and reports of minor mischiefs that were 'hardly worth recording'.[21] Anti-Japanese acts that featured among the reported 'minor mischiefs' were the organized boycott of agricultural produce from Nissa Shokai, the sole Japanese enterprise in the country, and the repeated cutting of the telephone line to its rubber estate at Samarahan.[22] When war in Europe flared in 1939, the Chinese, like other subjects of the Raj, contributed to the British war effort.

THE EUROPEANS

Largely as a consequence of Brooke policy and design, the number of Europeans was always small relative to the native population. As Table 1.1 illustrates, the Europeans were but a handful *vis-à-vis* the Chinese and indigenous inhabitants. The majority of Europeans served in the government bureaucracy, which itself was never elaborate and had but a skeletal staff. Brooke officers were ably assisted by Malay Native Officers in their dealings with the native inhabitants. Administrative paperwork was usually left to the Chinese court writer and other clerical staff, who were mostly Chinese or Eurasian and Sinhalese. The small knot of Europeans was further tightened during the reign of the Second White Rajah, Charles Anthoni Brooke (1868–1917), who was insistent on his rule that bachelor officers were preferred; wives and families, considered to be 'distractions', were greatly discouraged from settling in Sarawak. Furthermore, Brooke economic policies were generally prejudicial towards European investors lest these sophisticated (and, among them, unscrupulous) entrepreneurs take advantage and exploit the native peoples in the pursuit of profits. The Third White Rajah, Charles Vyner Brooke (1917–41), faithfully adhered to the traditional Brooke policy of protecting native interests against foreign (Chinese and European) encroachment. Rajah Vyner, in fact, was more partisan in upholding native welfare and rights than his father and predecessor, Rajah Charles. Consequently, European investments and participation were discouraged during the inter-war years of Rajah Vyner's reign.[23] These circumstances contributed to the small European community.

Apart from the bulk of Europeans who served in the Brooke government as administrators, others belonged to the personnel of the various Christian denominational missions who served in churches (priests, ministers) and schools (teachers, principals); as employees of European companies and banks (Borneo Company Limited, or BCL, and Sarawak Oilfields Limited) as managers, technical staff, and supervisors; and administrative staff of the handful of European-owned rubber plantations.

In December 1941, Sarawak was a picture of an untroubled, idyllic country in the tropics where indigenous and Chinese peasant smallholders of rice-fields, sago and rubber gardens, coconut groves, and fruit orchards, transported their produce in small wooden crafts utilizing the numerous rivers as the main mode of transportation to the bazaar. Overseeing the administration and guarding the peace was the much respected European Brooke officer, assisted by his trusted Malay Native Officer.

Therefore, when the Japanese invasion forces arrived on Sarawak soil, they found themselves faced with a country and people contented with eking out a livelihood from the land, largely oblivious to happenings (whether political or otherwise) in neighbouring territories, and generally satisfied with the governance of their White Rajah.

Notes

1. *Seventh Malaysia Plan 1996–2000* (Kuala Lumpur: Percetakan Nasional Malaysia, 1996) p. 139.
2. 'Order No. I-1 (Interpretation) 1933', *Sarawak Government Gazette (SGG)*, 1 July 1933, pp. 160, 164.
3. For Brooke paternalistic policy towards native peoples, see Ooi Keat Gin, *Of Free Trade and Native Interests: The Brookes and the Economic Development of Sarawak, 1841–1941* (Kuala Lumpur: Oxford University Press, 1997) pp. 225–50.

4. The *Datu Patinggi* and the *Datu Bandar* controlled the tribes on the left- and right-hand branch of the Sarawak River respectively, while the *Datu Temanggong* held sway over the inhabitants on the coast. See S. Baring-Gould and C. A. Bampfylde, *A History of Sarawak under its Two White Rajahs, 1839–1908* (London: Henry Sotheran, 1909) pp. 77–8, 82.

5. In 1855, acting upon the advice given by his friend and supporter, Lord Grey, a council of State called the Supreme Council was established by James which institutionalized the practice of consulting native opinion. See Brooke to Templer, 22 October 1855, in Gertrude L. Jacob, *The Raja of Sarawak: An Account of Sir James Brooke, K.C.B., LL.D., Given Chiefly Through Letters and Journals* (London: Macmillan, 1876) I, p. 211. For an account of the Supreme Council, see T. Stirling Boyd, 'The Law and Constitution of Sarawak' (Typescript), 1934, MSS Pac.s.86, Rhodes House Library (RHL), Box 4 Item II, pp. 29–32; and R. J. Pole-Evans, 'The Supreme Council, Sarawak', *Sarawak Museum Journal (SMJ)*, 7, 7 (June 1956) 98–108.

6. From 1931 and throughout the decade, Penghulu Asun of Entabai, Kanowit, conducted a protracted revolt against the Brooke government over the issue of tax collection. For this Iban uprising, see Steven Runciman, *The White Rajahs: A History of Sarawak from 1841 to 1946* (Cambridge: Cambridge University Press, 1960) pp. 239–40; and Robert Pringle, 'Asun's "Rebellion": The Political Growing Pains of a Tribal Society in Brooke Sarawak, 1929–1940', *SMJ*, 16, 32–3 (July–December 1968) 346–76.

7. For Malay education in Sarawak during the Brooke period, see Ooi Keat Gin, 'Sarawak Malay Attitudes Towards Education During the Brooke Period, 1841–1946', *Journal of Southeast Asian Studies (JSEAS)*, 21, 2 (September 1990) 340–59.

8. For the education of the non-Malay indigenous peoples during Brooke rule, see Ooi Keat Gin, 'Mission Education in Sarawak During the Period of Brooke Rule, 1841–1946', *SMJ*, 62, 63 (December 1991) 283–373.

9. There were a few Malay and Iban organizations established during the 1930s, namely The Persatuan Melayu Sarawak or Malay National Union (1939), Dayaks Co-operative Society (1939), The Sarawak Malay Savings and Investment Society (1940), and The Persekutuan Bumiputera Sarawak (1941). None of these organizations had a political agenda. See R. H. W. Reece, *The Name of Brooke: The End of White Rajah Rule in Sarawak* (Kuala Lumpur: Oxford University Press, 1982) pp. 132–9; and Sanib Said, *Malay Politics in Sarawak*

1946–1966: The Search for Unity and Political Ascendancy
(Singapore: Oxford University Press, 1985) pp. 28–9.

10.   For various perspectives on this conflict, see Runciman, *The
       White Rajahs*, pp. 119–33; Craig A. Lockard, 'The 1857
       Chinese Rebellion in Sarawak: A Reappraisal', *JSEAS*, 9, 1
       (March 1978) 85–98; and Graham Saunders, 'The Bau
       Chinese Attack on Kuching, February 1857: A Different
       Perspective', *SMJ*, 42, 63 (December 1991) 375–96.

11.   For the death penalty of the leader of a 'secret hueh', see
       Order dated 14 May 1870, 'Orders which have not since been
       cancelled, issued by H. H. the Rajah of Sarawak or with his
       sanction from 1863 to 1890 inclusive', Kuching, 1891, Sarawak
       Museum Archives (SMA); and *Sarawak Gazette (SG)*,
       24 January 1871, n.p. However, it has been pointed out that
       enforcement of such regulations was difficult, if not impossi-
       ble. For instance, see N. Denison, 'Notes on the Land Dyaks
       of Sarawak Proper', *SG*, 16 January 1877, p. 7. Such dracon-
       ian laws did not completely deter secret society activities,
       which emerged now and then: for example, during the
       unfavourable economic environment of the early 1930s. See
       SG, 1 September 1932, p. 158; *Sarawak Administration Report
       (SAR) 1932*, p. 14; *SG*, 1 May 1933, p. 66; *SG*, 2 January 1934,
       p. 2; and *SG*, 1 October 1935, p. 186.

12.   Apart from 'a solitary communist pamphlet' that was 'found
       stuck to a tree in Sibu in August' of 1936, no other indication
       of Leftist activities was uncovered in the country. See *SAR
       1936*, p. 27.

13.   *SAR 1934*, p. 18.

14.   For the regulation relating to naturalization, see 'Order
       No. XII, 1900', *SG*, 2 July 1900, pp. 128–9; 'Order N-2
       (Nationality and Naturalization)', *SGG*, 16 July 1934, pp. 344–8;
       and *SAR 1934*, p. 11.

15.   According to the population estimate carried out in 1939, the
       Chinese numbered 123 626 out of the total population of
       490 585. The growth in the Chinese population was more a
       result of natural increase than immigration. Land designated
       as 'Mixed Zone' accounted for slightly less than 5000 square
       miles of the total land area of 48 250 square miles. See J. L.
       Noakes, *Sarawak and Brunei: A Report on the 1947 Population
       Census* (Kuching: Government Printing Office, 1950) pp. 33,
       35, 40; and James C. Jackson, *Sarawak: A Geographical Survey
       of A Developing State* (London: University of London Press,
       1968) pp. 53, 74.

16.   Craig Alan Lockard, *From Kampung to City: A Social
       History of Kuching, Malaysia, 1820–1970* (Ohio University

Monographs in International Studies, Southeast Asia Series, No. 75, Athens, Ohio: Ohio University Press, 1987) p. 67.

17. During the early 1910s, Rajah Charles displayed his confidence and trust in Chinese communal leaders by endowing seven of them with magisterial powers to preside over a newly created Chinese Court. It was felt that the Chinese themselves would be in a far better position to handle matters relating to marriage and the division of properties where Chinese customary law and tradition applied. See *SG*, 17 April 1911, p. 67; *SG*, 16 June 1911, pp. 108–9; and Lockard, *Kampung to City*, pp. 52, 106.

18. See K. H. Digby, *Lawyer in the Wilderness* (Cornell University Southeast Asia Program Data Paper No. 114, Ithaca, New York: Cornell University Press, October 1980) p. 85.

19. John M. Chin, *The Sarawak Chinese* (Kuala Lumpur: Oxford University Press, 1981) p. 103. See also James R. Hipkins, 'The History of the Chinese in Borneo', *SMJ*, 19, 38–9 (July–December 1971) 125–46.

20. For Chinese anti-Japanese activities, see *SAR 1937*, pp. 34–5.

21. *SAR 1937*, p. 35.

22. Ibid, pp. 34–5; and Digby, *Lawyer in the Wilderness*, p. 33.

23. For Brooke socio-economic policies, see Ooi, *Of Free Trade and Native Interests*, pp. 19–79.

2 Japanese Pre-War Activities in North-West Borneo

As early as the years following the First World War (1914–18), the Japanese had taken an interest in the affairs of north-west Borneo. Like elsewhere in South-East Asia, there were Japanese immigrants in Sarawak and British North Borneo. Initially they came as individuals, generally in professions such as barber, dentist, physician and, for young female immigrants, as hairdressers and masseurs, but mostly as prostitutes in Japanese-owned and managed brothels. Some Japanese also became petty traders, market gardeners, or rubber plantation owners. Paralleling this individual emigration, several leading Japanese corporations had made large investments. A notable example was that of Mitsubishi, which was a major *zaibatsu* (conglomerate of companies) during the inter-war period; it had investments and commercial ventures throughout South-East Asia. The Mitsubishi Shoji Kaisha and its subsidiaries were engaged in a variety of commercial enterprises from managing rubber plantations to trade in consumer goods. Equally active was the Nissan group of companies. During the 1920s and 1930s, official trade missions were despatched to territories in South-East Asia to promote trade and commercial investments. Representatives of these huge corporations and members of trade missions enjoyed semi-official status with close links to Japanese embassies and consulates in the region.

In Sarawak, Japanese immigrants first arrived in Kuching in the later part of the 1880s. They were petty traders and street hawkers. Later arrivals during the early 1900s engaged in smallholdings, Para rubber cultivation and market gardening on the eastern fringes of the town. Others worked as

19

physicians, dentists, photographers and prostitutes in the bazaar.[1] Nissa Shokai, a trading firm specializing in Japanese goods, was established at the turn of the century, to cater for the needs of the then small Japanese community in Kuching and its outskirts. This firm was affiliated to a Japanese-owned Para rubber plantation in Samarahan. On this Samarahan estate, attempts were made to grow pineapples and other tropical cash crops. There were ambitious attempts to establish a Japanese rice-farming community during the late 1920s. However, the wet-rice cultivation undertaken by a small group of Japanese farming families on the Nissa Shokai property in the Upper Samarahan did not go beyond the experimental stage.[2]

The Japanese community in Sarawak remained a small minority numbering 155 (men, women and children) according to the 1939 Enumeration.[3] The Japanese individuals lived inconspicuously; Nissa Shokai also kept a low profile.

The situation in British North Borneo was different in that the Japanese community was larger, numbering more than 500 on the eve of the invasion; in fact, it had colonized almost an entire district (Tawau). Following the arrival of individuals after the First World War, the 1920s and 1930s witnessed an influx of Japanese agricultural peasant settlers and fishermen. The Borneo Fishery Company Limited, a Mitsubishi subsidiary subsidized by the Formosan government to the tune of one million yen, had branches in Sandakan, Tawau and on Banggi Island, and a fish canning factory on Si Amil Island near the entrance to Darvel Bay where a community of 300 Japanese lived and worked. Banggi Island was home to 160 fishermen. The Japanese fishing fleet possessed five fast diesel motor craft, three bait boats and two lighters; it employed the latest fishing techniques. This fishing operation was described as 'one of the most successful fishing enterprises in the South Seas' producing 'tinned and dried bonito'.[4] A Japanese agricultural colony flourished in the Tawau district with several estates and plantations collectively totalling 17 928 hectares (44 820 acres), producing rubber, coconuts, Manila hemp for the export markets, and vegetables for local consumption. The Nissan group had control over the Nippon Sangyo Gomu K. K. (Japan Industries Rubber Company) which owned several rubber estates in Tawau. Kuala Belait (in Brunei) had a smaller Japanese colony.[5]

In 1924 a Japanese trade mission under the auspices of the South Seas Association, but believed to be sponsored by the Japanese Foreign Office, visited North Borneo. The Japanese Consul at Sandakan had consular jurisdiction not only over British North Borneo but also exercised control over Brunei and Sarawak. It was believed that there existed a secret internal and external Japanese courier service.

The Japanese, as a whole, maintained a cordial and hospitable attitude towards the local government and population, particularly the indigenous peoples. In Kuching the Japanese courted the Malays; some even married Muslim Malay women, whilst others nominally embraced Islam. There was no doubt that Japanese consulate officials, representatives of commercial firms, and some Japanese individuals were spies. An Allied intelligence report cited the following observation:

> Members of Japanese commercial concerns as well as individually employed Japanese were disposed towards 'buying over' officials and others who might have been in possession of useful information or the means of obtaining it. The Japanese catered for the tastes of their 'prospects' – whether they were for money, women, drink or ambition. It was stated on reliable authority that costly Christmas presents were given to a few officials in some areas of B.N.B. [British North Borneo], but no comment was offered as to whether these overtures had the desired effect. (The desired effect, in this instance, probably was to establish cordial relations which would [preclude] the growth of suspicion).[6]

During the 1940–41 period, the Japanese showed a marked interest in north-west Borneo. In October 1940, the Japanese Consul at Sandakan embarked on a tour of British North

Borneo, Brunei, and Sarawak. Although all these territories were rightfully under his consular jurisdiction, it was quite obvious that this mission was aimed at 'selecting suitable landing places for an invading force'.[7]

In 1937, the Japanese government established a think-tank organization known as the Institute to Promote Pacific Relations, or *Showa Kenkyukai*. The economic advantages of Borneo, and particularly its oil fields, were highlighted by the *Showa Kenkyukai*. Its members were instrumental in advocating imperial designs over Borneo.[8] A prominent example was that of Koichiro Ishihara, who emphasized the economic importance of Borneo. Ishihara owned a newspaper, the *Osaka Jiji*, which became a mouthpiece for his southward expansionist rhetoric. His books, *The Building of New Japan* (1934) and *Japan at the Crossroads* (1940), advocated the southward expansion policy. Ishihara's writings, together with those of other members of the *Showa Kenkyukai*, to a certain extent influenced planners in the Japanese military.[9]

JAPAN'S SOUTHWARD EXPANSION POLICY

Planners in the Japanese military during the years leading to the attack on Pearl Harbor had outlined strategies and made preparations in the event of advancement and occupation of *Nampo*, the 'Southern Area' (that is, the countries of South-East Asia). The ultimate objective was to establish a new order in East Asia, namely the Greater East Asia Co-Prosperity Sphere. These plans were continuously revised and pruned; when activated, the General Officer Commanding the Southern Army, in cooperation with the Navy, was immediately to proceed to occupy essential areas, such as the Philippines, British Malaya, the Dutch East Indies and part of Burma.[10] Meanwhile, no disturbance was expected from Thailand and/or French Indo-China; in the event that the Thai and/or French Indo-Chinese armies 'resist[ed]', these two territories were also to 'be fully occupied'.[11]

The strategic importance of Sarawak and north-west Borneo lies in the economically vital oil fields which were one of the prime targets for the southward expansion policy. The oil fields were located at Miri in Sarawak, and also some thirty-two miles northwards, at Seria in Brunei territory. The crude oil from both fields was pumped through pipelines to the refinery at Lutong on the Sarawak coast, whence sea loading lines pumped the oil to tankers off the coast.

JAPAN'S CRITICAL OIL SITUATION

To the Americans it seemed that Japan was being denied oil which would increase its powers of military aggression; to the Japanese it seemed their country was being forced towards military aggression through failure of their peaceful moves to increase their oil supplies.[12]

Japan's domestic output of crude oil supplied only about 10 per cent of its yearly consumption, while the rest of its requirements relied on imports from abroad. The usual suppliers were the USA (more than 80 per cent), and the Dutch East Indies (about 10 per cent), with the remainder from other sources. From the mid-1930s the Japanese government had initiated plans for increasing storage facilities and refining capacity, both part of war planning policy, 'the increased storage to enable her to carry over the period of conquest and exploitation of the oil resources captured, and the increased refining capacity to handle the flow from the captured oilfields'.[13] Reserves were built up from 30 million barrels in 1934 to over 51 million barrels in 1939.[14]

Despite all efforts to increase the oil supply, there were still deficits which had to be met by captured oil fields in the Southern Area. Therefore, British Borneo and the Dutch East Indies were strategically economic primary objectives in the southward expansion policy as well as vital components of the Greater East Asia Co-Prosperity Sphere.

Notes

1. See Craig Alan Lockard, *From Kampung to City: A Social History of Kuching, Malaysia, 1820–1970* (Ohio University Monographs in International Studies, Southeast Asia Series, No. 75, Athens, Ohio: Ohio University Press, 1987) pp. 38, 44, 86, 90, 96, 143.

2. See *SAR 1929*, p. 22; *SG*, 2 January 1936, p. 16; *SG*, 1 April 1936, p. 87; and C. L. Newman, *Report on Padi in Sarawak* (Kuching: Government Printing Office, 1938) pp. 8–9.

3. In fact, 'Japanese' is not even listed as one of the ethnic groups under the general heading of 'Other Non-Indigenous Asiatic' which included 'Indian', 'Ceylonese', 'Javanese', 'Bugis', 'Filipino' and 'Others' (Arabs, Bataks, Banjorese, Siamese, Javanese [?]). See J. L. Noakes, *Sarawak and Brunei: A Report on the 1947 Population Census* (Kuching: Government Printing Press, 1950) pp. 35, 40.

4. Eric Robertson, *The Japanese File: Pre-War Japanese Penetration in Southeast Asia* (Singapore: Heinemann Asia, 1979) p. 56.

5. See 'British Territories in North Borneo', extract from Allied Land Forces South-East Asia (A.L.F.S.E.A.), Wartime Intellegence Report (W.I.R.), No. 52, 28 September 1945 (War Office, or WO 208/105, Public Record Office, or PRO) pp. 16–17, 19–20.

6. Ibid., p. 20.

7. Robertson, *Japanese File*, p. 126.

8. See Joyce C. Lebra, *Japan's Greater East Asia Co-Prosperity Sphere in World War II: Selected Readings and Documents* (Kuala Lumpur: Oxford University Press, 1975) pp. 44–5, 64–7, 99–103, 116–17. See also John Robertson, *Australia at War 1939–1945* (Melbourne: William Heinemann, 1981) pp. 62–3, 68–9; and S. Woodburn Kirby *et al.*, *The War Against Japan Vol. I: The Loss of Singapore* (London: Her Majesty's Stationery Office, or HMSO, 1957) pp. 477–8, 481–3.

9. In the preface to his *Japan at the Crossroads*, Ishihara boasted 'that a part of his views had already been adopted by the present [Japanese] Cabinet', cited in Robertson, *Japanese File*, p. 5.

10. 'Orders Relating to the Occupation of the Vital Southern Area', Special Intelligence Bulletin: Japanese Plans and Operation in S.E. Asia – Translation of Japanese Documents, 21 December 1945 (W0 203/6310, PRO) Document 2.

11. Ibid.

12. Robertson, *Australia at War*, p. 63.

13. Kirby, *The War Against Japan*, p. 481.

14. Ibid.

3 Invasion and Occupation

According to Japanese military thinking, Borneo possessed economic as well as strategic importance. As already mentioned, the economically essential oil fields at Miri (Sarawak), Seria (Brunei), Tarakan and Balikpapan (Dutch Borneo) were prime targets. The island of Borneo, equidistant for bombing raids from both British Malaya and Dutch Java, made its capture a fundamental prerequisite to successful operations in these two erritories. Furthermore, the occupation of Borneo was essential to securing control over the south-west Pacific. The strategic position of the island of Borneo is obvious: it is centrally located between the main sea routes of South-East Asia, namely the Straits of Malacca to the north which guarded British Malaya and Dutch Sumatra on the one hand, and the Sulu Sea and the Java Sea, which protected the greater part of Dutch East Indies, particularly the Celebes and Java respectively. More important from the military standpoint was the north-west coastline of Borneo, which covered the approaches to Singapore and British Malaya by way of the South China Sea. Along this stretch of coast were located the British protectorates of Sarawak, Brunei and British North Borneo which should have been well-equipped to defend the sea lanes (see Map 3.1).

Although Borneo was appreciated as 'part of the outer defences of Malaya',[1] both the British and Dutch authorities had insufficient resources to capitalise on this strategic advantage. Ironically the British protectorates of Sarawak, Brunei and British North Borneo could not even protect themselves, let alone protect the sea approaches to Singapore and British Malaya.

Map 3.1   Strategic position of North-West Borneo (Sarawak, Brunei, British North Borneo) in the 'Southern Area'

△ Kuching 7th Mile (Bukit Stabar) Landing Ground

▲ I Singkawang II Aerodrome

FACING THE ENEMY: SARAWAK'S DEFENCE PREPARATIONS

As early as the 1850s, James Brooke had argued on countless occasions that Sarawak could not stand on its own but needed a 'protective power' against predatory countries. He sought this protection from his home country but was shunned; likewise feelers sent to the governments of the Netherlands, Belgium, France and Italy were equally unsuccessful. Finally, in 1863 Great Britain granted recognition of Sarawak as an independent and sovereign country. 'Protection', however, 'was not accorded till 1888', during the reign of Rajah Charles, 'and then it was offered, not asked for, and was granted, not in the interests of Sarawak, but for safeguarding of Imperial interests, lest some other foreign power should lay its hands on the little State'.[2] Therefore, under the 1888 Agreement with Great Britain, all relations of Sarawak with foreign countries were to be conducted by Her Majesty's government which would undertake to protect it from without. Internal administration remained in the hands of the Brooke Rajahs.[3]

In accordance with this Agreement, Britain undertook to despatch troops and equipment to Sarawak during the late 1930s when it was generally certain that war in the East was inevitable. Britain's effort in rendering military assistance was pathetic to say the least.

Throughout the 1930s Sarawak was being visited by several seaplanes and flying boats of the 205th Squadron of the Royal Air Force based in Singapore. Interest within official circles in aviation adopted a positive note with the arrival of C. W. Bailey, Works and Building Inspector of the Royal Air Force (RAF), Singapore, who offered his professional assistance in the planning and construction of airstrips in the country. In 1935 the Brooke government decided to conduct the preliminary work of establishing airstrips at selected sites throughout the country, namely at Kuching, Oya, Mukah, Bintulu and Miri.[4] Work began on the construction of the Kuching, Miri and Bintulu landing strips; the Bintulu airstrip, however, was discontinued in October 1938. On 26 September 1938, the Kuching landing ground situated at the 7th Mile (Bukit Stabar) measuring 'seven hundred yards by three hundred yards wide', it was officially opened with much fanfare.[5] But no military aircraft were stationed on Sarawak soil. Likewise, the Royal Navy was absent in the waters off north-west Borneo where three protectorates of Great Britain were located.

Despite Sarawak's strategic position on the north-western fringe of Borneo with its oil fields and a viable landing ground near Kuching,[6] for want of resources British military planners advocated scorched earth tactics in place of defence. It was suggested that Britain and her allies had ample time between the outbreak of war with Germany in September 1939 and the assault on Pearl Harbor in December 1941 to prepare plans to face the widely predicted Japanese offensive in South-East Asia.[7] But the main reason for the unpreparedness in the colonies when war clouds broke was that Britain did not have the money, men and equipment to protect her vast empire. The Singapore Conference of October 1940 which considered the possibility of the Japanese seizing British Borneo, argued that without command of the sea it was pointless to defend the strategic bases. Alternatively, it was suggested that air superiority of 200 planes was sufficient for protecting British and Dutch Borneo.[8] However, Britain did not have the resources to command either the sea or the sky.

The contingency plan of activating a denial scheme was in fact the most realistic under the circumstances of inadequate resources. Denial schemes were in place to render the oil installations at Miri and Lutong unusable to the enemy. Likewise, the Bukit Stabar Landing Ground, 11 kilometres (8 miles) to the south of Kuching town, was to be held as long as possible, failing which its destruction was to be effected.

The only military force Britain could afford to deploy for Sarawak's defence, under the 1888 agreement, was one Indian 1050-member infantry battalion, the 2nd Battalion of the 15th Punjab Regiment (herein 2nd/15th Punjab) under the command of Major (later Lieutenant Colonel) C. M. Lane. One infantry company with a detachment of one six-inch battery and a demolition squad of Royal Engineers was stationed at Miri; they were entrusted with the task of executing the oil field denial scheme. The Miri Detachment, consisting of two officers and 98 Indian other ranks, arrived at Miri on 23 December 1940. The remainder of the forces (the Kuching Detachment of one officer and 52 Indian other ranks) was deployed to defend the airstrip outside Kuching. 'Tactically', Major Lane frankly admitted, 'the [Kuching] detachment had no value, but its bluff and propaganda value might, it was thought, slow up an attack and stiffen the morale of the civil demolition parties'.[9] To complement the British troops, the Brooke government had mobilized its civil servants, the Sarawak Rangers,[10] and other voluntary bodies for the defence of the country. Altogether SARFOR (Sarawak Forces), consisting of 2nd/15th Punjab Regiment and all local Sarawak and Brunei forces, numbered in total 2565 officers and other ranks.[11]

Initially, a plan for mobile defence (Plan 'A'), which aimed at holding the landing ground at Kuching for as long as possible, and to hold off the Japanese till the denial schemes could be executed completely, was proposed. In the event that the advance of the enemy could not be halted, the landing ground could be destroyed and the entire force could retreat in small parties into the surrounding hills and jungles to carry on guerilla warfare in an attempt to deny the use of the airstrip. However, at the Anglo-Dutch military officers conference in Kuching in September 1941, it was pointed out that SARFOR could not carry out Plan 'A' if the Japanese landed 3000–4000 forces with air and sea support. J. L. Noakes, Sarawak Secretary for Defence, had persistently argued along these lines regarding the inadequacy of SARFOR, and had appealed to Malaya Command at Singapore for more troops and equipment.[12]

British military planners at Singapore, responsible for the defence of three British Borneo territories, were clearly aware of the prevailing inadequacy of defence measures. The

General Officer Commanding Malaya, Lieutenant-General A. E. Percival, following a two-day tour of Kuching in late November 1941, summarized the situation as follows:

> Nobody could pretend that this was a satisfactory situation, but at least it would make the enemy deploy a bigger force to capture the place than would have been necessary if it had not been defended at all and that, I think, is the true way to look at it ... The best I could do was to promise to send them a few anti-aircraft guns and to tell them of the arrival of the [battleship] *Prince of Wales* and [battle-cruiser] *Repulse*, which were due at Singapore in a few days' time – not that I expected the anti-aircraft guns to be of much practical value but I felt that the moral effect of their presence there would more than counterbalance some slight dispersion of force.[13]

Consequently, an alternative plan of action, Plan 'B', based on static defence, was set out. All the available troops and stores were to be concentrated within the 5.5 kilometre (3.5 mile) perimeter of the airstrip to ensure that its destruction was not interfered with. The rationale for Plan 'B' was succintly presented by Air Chief Marshal Sir Robert Brooke-Popham, Commander-in-Chief in the Far East:

> The only place which it was decided to hold was Kuching, the reason for this being not only that there was an aerodrome at that place, but that its occupation by the enemy might give access to the aerodromes in Dutch Borneo at the north-western end of the island, these aerodromes being only some 350 miles from Singapore, i.e. much nearer than any in South Indo-China.[14]

In spite of the general weaknesses and shortcomings of defence measures, which were known to most of Rajah Vyner's senior officers, it was commendable on their part to agree that they should all remain at their posts at all cost instead of a complete evacuation in the face of an invasion. The plan to remain at their respective posts was conceived as early as June 1941, followed by confirmation of these orders on 1 December. 'It was clearly pointed out', according to 'definite instructions' issued by the Chief Secretary, Cyril Drummond Le Gros Clark,[15] 'that officers in charge of districts were expected to remain at their stations provided that, if the inhabitants of any district moved en masse then the Officer in Charge of the Station would be at liberty to follow'.[16] Such instructions was clearly in tandem with Brooke tradition whereby the protection of the interests of the people of Sarawak was paramount; as officers of the Raj it was imperative that they should be present with the local people to face the enemy together. Le Gros Clark was adamant that 'it was his duty, in the absence of His Highness the Rajah, to stand by the people'; consequently he declined the suggestion that he personally withdraw with the Military Headquarters when the need arose so as to facilitate the functioning of the Sarawak civil government elsewhere in Borneo.[17]

THE INVASION

Between 15 December 1941, which saw the Japanese invasion force off Tanjong Baram (Baram Point), to the surrender of Kuching on Christmas Eve, a period of less than ten days, Brooke Sarawak came under Japanese control and became part of Imperial Japan's empire.

On 13 December 1941, a Japanese convoy left Cam Ranh Bay in French Vietnam and headed for north-west Borneo. It consisted of the 35th Infantry Brigade of the 124th Infantry Regiment under the command of Major-General Kiyotake Kawaguchi (referred to as the 'Kawaguchi Detachment')[18] and the 2nd Yokosuka Naval Landing Force flanked by an escort of cruisers and destroyers with two seaplanes for reconnaissance. The battle plan outlined was as follows:

a landing would be made at Miri and Seria to capture and secure the oilfield district and airfields in that area. A large part of the force would then re-establish the Miri oilfield while the main body was to capture the Kuching airbase.[19]

When war broke out with Japan following the attack on Pearl Harbor in the Hawaiian Islands on 8 December 1941, the authorities in Sarawak activated all measures for the defence of the country. Three days prior to the Miri landings, the full denial schemes[20] at the oil fields were effectively executed. The most significant action was the implementation of the various denial schemes, namely disabling the oil installations and the landing grounds. The 'Permanent Denial Scheme' of the oil fields was carried out from 8 to 11 December 1941 by employees of Sarawak Oilfields Limited, with the assistance of personnel from the Detachment of Royal Engineers and Loyals. This scheme consisted of the removal of essential parts to Singapore. On 12 December, denial work commenced on the Miri Landing Ground. In the case of the landing ground, however, only partial damage was effected. Meanwhile, at Lutong, a double-check was carried out on the permanent destruction of the sea oil loading lines where submarine charges were attached; it was pronounced 'completely successful'.[21]

On 15 December, the invasion force anchored off Tanjong Baram (Baram Point). The choppy sea delayed the landings as the increased wind velocity and the high waves prevented the smooth transfer of troops from ship to landing barge. Finally in the early hours of dawn of 16 December, the Japanese landed on Sarawak soil.

> There was very little resistance from the enemy and, during the morning of the 16th [December 1941], the two units captured the oilfields at Seria [Brunei] and oilfields and airfield at Miri. The 2nd Special Naval Landing Force of the Yokosuka Naval District landed near the Miri airfield. It then proceeded to occupy and secure the field without meeting any resistance.[22]

The main body of the Detachment entered Miri town where about 50 members of the local police unit awaited them. The latter surrendered without much trouble. Apparently the invaders had 40 casualties, mostly drownings owing to the difficult sea conditions during the transfer of troops from the ships to the landing barges.[23]

TUANS DAN MEMS LARI: THE FLIGHT OF
EUROPEAN MEN AND WOMEN

A week prior to the Japanese landings evacuation by sea was effected for the oil industry personnel and Brooke civil servants and their families.[24] Chinese and indigenous inhabitants witnessed with surprise the hurried exodus of the White 'Tuans' and 'Mems'. European inhabitants in the outstations generally proceeded inland to evade capture by the enemy. Good sense, however, prevailed over the hopelessness of their attempts to flee to the relatively unknown interior; subsequently most of them surrendered to the Japanese. They were interned at Batu Lintang Internment Camp, Kuching.

Nevertheless, some individuals did manage to escape to Pontianak, awaiting transfer to Java and thence to Australia. The overland journey from Bau to Pontianak was precarious jungle trekking. The few determined Europeans who made it met up with Dutch evacuees at Pontianak to await the evacuation of European civilians to Java. A fortunate few managed the dash to freedom all the way to Australia; however, among them, they left behind husbands and sons to face the Japanese invaders.

Although most Brooke officers upheld their duty and remained at their posts as instructed by the Chief Secretary, those in the Third Division fled helter-skelter. It is difficult to ascertain whether the Christmas and Boxing Day aerial bombings of Sibu sparked a panic among the local inhabitants that went out of control with lootings and chaos, or whether the evacuation of the Resident and his officers together with other Europeans (staff of BCL, missions, etc.) caused the turbulent and riotous situation. Clearly a breakdown of government and control was evident in the Lower Rejang. 'It would appear', wrote Noakes, 'that from 25th [December] onwards all European control disappeared'.[25] There was a strong anti-European feeling in the region. Such collective expressions of resentment amongst the native and Chinese population were hitherto practically unheard of. Contemporary European observers felt the hurried departure of Europeans including the Resident himself, A. Macpherson, was the chief cause: W. G. Morison, ADO, Sarikei, noted 'a strong feeling of resentment against all Europeans in Sarikei at that time [24 January 1942]',[26] while Mr G. D. Kidd, manager of Rejang Estates Limited, lamented that the 'flight of Europeans in December 1941 was a deplorable action ... [and there was] a feeling of antagonism towards Europeans which will be difficult to eradicate in future years'.[27] The Kidds refused to evacuate until subsequently arrested by the Japanese and deported to Kuching.

'THE TOWN OF KUCHING WAS OCCUPIED WITHOUT ANY RESISTANCE'

Meanwhile in Kuching, the greater part of the defence measures were put into action. Apparently there was a breakdown in communication among certain parties in the civilian defence set-up, but more telling was the non-coordination of action between the civil service volunteers and military personnel. Consequently, many groups were cut off from one another. One by one, European government officers, including the Chief Secretary himself, were rounded up by the Japanese.

There was apparently a breakdown in communication between the civil authorities and their military counterparts owing to the destruction of telephone lines as a consequence of the implementation of denial of the Direction Finding Station (DFS).[28] According to the military commander, the Charge-Hand-in-Charge, Mr Henley-Joy, was given the task of destroying the DFS by fire. Apparently this instruction was not made known to the civil authorities for neither the Chief Secretary nor the Secretary for Defence knew of such a denial scheme. It was argued by the Secretary for Defence that had the civil authorities been warned of such an occurrence, the Postmaster-General, who was in charge of the telephone and other communication facilities, would have taken precautionary measures to safeguard the telephone wires. As a result of this communications severance, vital information about enemy movements received by the civil authorities could not be taken advantage of by the military.

Furthermore, in the absence of information about enemy movements, and more importantly, the quick dissemination of such information to all SARFOR units, the 'surprise' element would not have benefited the Japanese to any great extent. Literally many sections of the defenders were 'caught with their pants down'; for instance, many vehicles were captured in perfect running condition, and the non-immobilisation of transmitting sets by removing and destroying essential parts are but two examples of Japanese 'surprise'.[29]

Ignorance of enemy movements is one thing, but to refuse to believe the quick pace of the Japanese advance, particularly their landings at Santubong, a short distance to the north-west of Kuching, was paid for dearly by the military commander. If Major Lane had taken the Santubong landings more seriously, he might have altered his strategy thereby giving him more time to effect a more successful retreat into Dutch Borneo. An underestimation of enemy strength and, perhaps, plain arrogance, coloured the British military commander's attitude towards the Japanese advance.

Eight days after the fall of Miri, at 4 o'clock on the afternoon of Christmas Eve, Kuching surrendered. There was scarcely any fighting and few casualties involved with the fall of Kuching to Japanese forces.

The majority of Brooke officers remained at their post; subsequently they were all rounded up:

[J. Beville Archer] with several other Europeans, was arrested, tied up and left for a day and night without food or water. They were then marched through the streets of Kuching as living symbols of the defeat of the white man, but if the Japanese expected the crowds of natives and Chinese to jeer at their captives they were disappointed ... as the small band of weary unshaven and dirty Europeans plodded through the streets there was dead silence and the people in the streets looked the other way.[30]

Brooke officers and other Europeans were sent to the internment camp at Batu Lintang, on the outskirts of Kuching.

Following the occupation of Kuching, the 2nd/15th Punjab retreated into Dutch Borneo, fighting a rearguard action; finally, on 3 April 1942, they too surrendered, and were subsequently brought back for imprisonment at Batu Lintang.[31]

Notes

1. A. E. Percival, *The War in Malaya* (London: Eyre & Spottiswoode, 1949) p. 62.
2. S. Baring-Gould and C. A. Bampfylde, *A History of Sarawak under its Two White Rajahs, 1839–1908* (London: Henry Sotheran, 1909) p. 301.
3. See Article 1 'Agreement between Her Majesty's Government and Charles Brooke, Second Rajah Of Sarawak', 5 September 1888, reproduced as Appendix B in Anthony Brooke, *The Facts About Sarawak: A Documented Account of the Cession to Britain in 1946* (Bombay, 1947; reprinted Singapore: Summer Times, 1983).
4. See *SAR 1935*, p. 21.
5. See *SAR 1938*, p. 1.
6. This airstrip was also referred to as the Bukit Stabar Landing Ground by virtue of its location at the 7th Milestone south of Kuching town.
7. See K. D. Shargava and K. N. V. Sastri, *Official History of the Indian Armed Forces in the Second World War, 1939–45: Campaigns in South-East Asia, 1941–42* (Combined Inter-Services Historical Section India and Pakistan, City Orient Longmans, 1960) p. 365.
8. Ibid., pp. 365–6. For details of pre-war Anglo-Dutch discussions see '[British] Staff discussions with Netherlands East Indies at Singapore in 1940. Staff conversations with officers from NEI [Netherlands East Indies], Memorandum drawn up by Conference on operation between British and Dutch Forces in event of Japanese attack on Malaya, Borneo or Netherlands East Indies, 1941' (AWM54 213/1/3, Australian War Memorial Archives (AWMA)); and 'British Staff conversation with Netherlands East Indies officers on co-operation in event of

Japanese attack on Malaya, Borneo or Netherlands East Indies, 26–29 1940' (AWM54 243/5/35, AWMA).

9. Colonel C. M. Lane, 'A Report on Operations in Sarawak and Dutch Borneo', p. 4, cited in Shargava and Sastri, *Indian Armed Forces*, p. 368.

10. The Sarawak Rangers, formed in 1846, was the only trained army of the Sarawak Raj. Its members were mostly Ibans who were trained and led by European officers.

11. See Shargava and Sastri, *Indian Armed Forces*, p. 370.

12. See J. L. Noakes, 'Report Upon Defence Measures Adopted in Sarawak from June 1941 to the Occupation in December 1941 by Imperial Japanese Forces; also, an account of the movement of British and Sarawak Military Forces during the Japanese invasion of Sarawak', 15 February 1946 (MSS Pac. s. 62, RHL) pp. 23–5.

    For a detailed treatment of the issue of the inadequacy of SARFOR, see Ooi Keat Gin, 'Broken Promise?': Great Britain's Failure to Honour Treaty Obligations to Brooke Sarawak, a British Protectorate', 18th Annual Conference of the Association of Southeast Asian Studies in the United Kingdom (ASEASUK), School of Oriental and African Studies, University of London, London, U.K., 1–3 April 1998.

13. Percival, *The War in Malaya*, p. 94.

14. Despatch by Air Chief Marshall Sir Robert Brooke-Popham, Commander-in-Chief in the Far East, on *Operations in the Far East from 17 October 1940 to 27 December 1941* (Supplement to the London Gazette, 20 January 1948) p. 538, cited in Shargava and Sastri, *Indian Armed Forces*, p. 373.

15. Le Gros Clark was appointed Chief Secretary from May 1941 following the retirement of J. B. Archer.

16. Noakes, 'Report Upon Defence Measures', Section V, p. 15.

17. Ibid. However, it was agreed that 'The Treasurer, Judicial Commissioner and Deputy Secretary for Defence were authorised to leave Kuching directly upon threat of invasion.'

18. This unit was under the overall command of the 18th Division (Lieutenant-General Renya Mutaguchi) which was responsible for operations in British Malaya; this Kawaguchi Detachment was entrusted with operations in British Borneo. See Shargava and Sastri, *Indian Armed Forces*, pp. 411–12.

19. Colonel Itsu Ogawa and Lieutenant-Colonel Ino Sei, 'Borneo Operations (Kawaguchi Detachment) 1941–1942', Japanese Studies in World War II (Box 6 AL 1099, Imperial War Museum, or IWM) p. 254.

20. As early as August 1941, partial implementation of the denial scheme had effectively reduced production by 70 per cent. See

Lionel Wigmore, *The Japanese Thrust* (Canberra: Australian War Memorial, 1957) pp. 179–80.

21. See Noakes, 'Report Upon Defence Measures', Section XVI, pp. 29–30.

22. 'Borneo Operations 1941–1945', Japanese Monograph No. 26, Headquarters United States Army Japan, Office of the Military History Officer, Foreign Histories Division, 20 November 1957 (Box 22 AL 5256, IWM) p. 8.

23. Ibid., p. 9.

24. For this sea evacuation from Miri to Kuching, see Noakes, 'Report Upon Defence Measures', Section XVIII, pp. 33–4.

25. Ibid., Section XXIV, p. 91.

26. Ibid., Section XXIV, p. 92.

27. Ibid., Section XXIV, p. 98.

28. See ibid., Section XX, p. 44.

29. See ibid., Section XVII, pp. 31–2; Section XX, pp. 44–5.

30. 'Autobiography of C. F. C. Macaskie', Papers of C. F. C. Macaskie (MSS Pac s. 71, RHL) pp. 141–2.

31. For the operations of the 2nd/15th Punjab, see Shargava and Sastri, *Indian Armed Forces*, pp. 374–80; Percival, *War in Malaya*, pp. 165–75; and A. V. M. Horton, 'A Note on the British Retreat from Kuching, 1941-1942', *SMJ*, 36, 57 (December 1986) 241–9.

According to Lionel Wigmore, the 2nd/15th Punjab Regiment was 'compelled to surrender on 9th March'; Horton, however, maintained that the remnants of the Regiment organized themselves into guerilla units in South Borneo to harass the enemy, and these men only gave up the struggle on 3 April after the fall of Java when all Allied forces were compelled to surrender. See Wigmore, *The Japanese Thrust*, p. 181, n. 5; and Horton, 'British Retreat', p. 246.

4 Under the Rising Sun

On the whole the inhabitants of Sarawak were more bewildered by the Japanese invasion and subsequent occupation than frightened of their new masters. The scant fighting with the retreating British defenders and the absence of physical resistance from the local population made the Japanese entry into Sarawak a fairly easy accomplishment. There were several civilian casualties in Kuching and the Lower Rejang district as a consequence of air raids prior to the landings, but little damage to property.[1]

All European inhabitants throughout Sarawak were rounded up, in most cases without resistance, and were brought to Kuching for internment in the main civilian camp at Batu Lintang, about five kilometres south of Kuching town. Allied prisoners-of-war (POWs) including Australians, British, Indians and Dutch, were imprisoned at Batu Lintang Camp, on Labuan Island, and at Sandakan and Jesselton in British North Borneo. The local inhabitants, apart from shortages and other economic hardships, were generally unmolested by the occupying forces.

THE *GUNSEIBU* GOVERNMENT

The policies of military government and administrative procedures in the occupied territories were laid out by the Tokyo planners; Japanese field commanders and their civilian counterparts were expected to execute these policies and procedures in their respective domains. Based on a captured Japanese document entitled 'The Administration of the Occupied Territories in the Vital Southern Area', dated 25 November 1941, the main objectives of establishing a military government 'are to plan the speedy acquisition of resources for homeland defence, the restoration of law and

39

order, to devise means of making the army of occupation self-supporting and to contribute to the success of the war'.[2] Under the sub-heading 'The Discovery and Acquisition of Resources', the document laid out the following: 'to devise speedy methods for the exploitation and acquisition of resources necessary for waging war and for Homeland Defence, and to plan the expansion of the Empire's military power'; 'to use supervised civilian labour in the acquisition of these vital resources. Selection of these civilians will be made after consultation with the appropriate branch of the central authorities', and 'The army will do its utmost to assist in the transporting of materials back to JAPAN, and will use all available commandeered shipping for this purpose.'[3]

Sarawak, Brunei and British North Borneo were governed as one military unit by the Japanese 37th Army with its headquarters at Kuching.[4] For administrative expediency, five provinces were created: *Kuching-shu* (Sarawak), *Sibu-shu* (Rejang and Central Sarawak), *Miri-shu* (Brunei and North Sarawak), *Seikai-shu* (Jesselton/West Coast State), and *Tokai-shu* (Sandakan/East Coast State). Each had a Japanese Provincial Governor.[5] The Japanese were content with controlling the coastal regions and settlements on the major rivers. Apart from occasional patrols, the interior districts were left relatively 'ungoverned'.

A military government, *Gunseibu*, was established. The sinking of four transports carrying Japanese civil affairs staff resulted in the almost complete domination of military personnel in all branches of the administration.[6] A policy of indirect rule was adopted, as exemplified in the predominantly Iban areas of the Second Division where a few educated Ibans in the Brooke bureaucracy were retained in their post or elevated to higher positions of authority. For instance, Eliab Bay (Bayang), an Iban was appointed liaison officer in Iban affairs by the *Gunseibu*. Such appointments as well as the retention of native police personnel (mostly Malays) and Brooke Native Officers (also for the most part Malays, with a few Ibans) by the Japanese were partly the result of expediency and, to a certain extent, partly politically motivated, in order to incorporate natives in the administration. In many

Plate 4.1 Marquis Toshinari Maeda, first Japanese military commander of northern Borneo (*courtesy Madam Yayako Maeda*)

parts of the country, the pre-war administration was maintained excluding the presence of the European officer. The Native Officer, often a Malay, assumed full control, subject only to the occasional visit by his Japanese superior. The

Plate 4.2   Japanese military administration staff, Kuching, 1943
(*courtesy Professor R. H. W. Reece*)

situation in Kanowit and Lawas was representative of other districts.[7] Likewise, the shortage of administrative staff also influenced the decision to utilize European personnel, releasing them from internment, in such essential services as 'medical, police, water supply, and food production'.[8] Overall the pre-war administrative structure was retained with principal positions reserved for Japanese. In order to supplement and to support the administrative machinery, the *Gunseibu* formed Japanese-sponsored organizations to fulfil certain political and military objectives.

Ken Sanjikai, or Prefectural Advisory District Councils, were established in each provincal centre. Each Council consisted of five to ten natives (Malay and Iban), mostly community leaders, appointed by the Governor of the Province acting upon the recommendation of the Japanese District Chief. Chinese, Indians, and other immigrants were appointed as Special Councillors. The *ken-sanji* (Councillors) were expected to hold bi-annual meetings under the chairmanship of the District Chief.[9] Administration in the outlying districts and the interior was left in the hands of native police personnel and village headmen. 'The system', as a post-war document summarizes the Japanese administration, 'is one of decentralised power allowing participation by local inhabitants under Japanese supervision'.[10]

Gunseibu-sponsored organizations like the *kyodotai*, a local militia, recruited mostly from Malays and Ibans, and wholly excluded Chinese. The Chinese were barred from acceptance into this organization by the commander of the 37th Army for obvious security reasons, and 'there were no exceptions' to this ruling.[11]

The *jikeidan*, a kind of vigilante corps, organized the local inhabitants into units of ten, thirty, and one hundred households with their respective leaders responsible to the local police. Longhouses constituted the *jikeidan* unit in the upriver areas.[12] In practice, householders functioned as an informal spy network reporting directly to the police.

Malay and Chinese schools conducted *Nippon-go* (Japanese language) classes.[13] Rituals such as daily exercises, the singing of the Japanese national anthem while facing in the direction of Japan, bowing to the picture of the Japanese emperor and observing Japanese festivals particularly the emperor's birthday, were all inculcated. 'Cultural shows', engaging school children to sing Japanese songs and perform for the entertainment of Japanese officers and local people, were staged as a public relations exercise with the aim of improving relations between the Japanese authorities and their newly conquered subjects. On such occasions, local community leaders were invited to deliver pro-Japanese speeches to the audience.

In Kuching, a Chinese Economic Board was constituted involving most of the leading Chinese *towkay*. Its objective was to defeat black-marketeering and smuggling.[14] A multi-ethnic Women's Board was established to raise funds for the Japanese war effort by demanding that its members, who were prominent women from the various ethnic groups, 'go among the women of their own race and persuade them to give up gold, silver and valuables to the Japanese government'.[15] This undertaking was generally carried out.

It is uncertain, however, whether similar organizations operated outside Kuching, but the Japanese-sponsored Overseas
Chinese Association established in Kuching had branches or
counterparts throughout the country. For instance, in Sibu it
was represented by the Joint Peace Keeping Association.[16]

In October 1942, a three-point objective was formulated as
the policy of the military government in occupied territories.
This document states that:

> For the present [1942] our policy in the development of
> this area [North Borneo] will be as follows:
>
> (a) Our plans at present are to use native princes as the
>   instruments of military government, according to their
>   former status and ability.
> (b) We must maintain the use of a part of the local vital
>   resources, particularly oil, as reserve stocks.
> (c) The political power of local Chinese must be restricted
>   as soon as possible.[17]

The adoption and implementation of these objectives will be
discussed in the following sections.

JAPANESE POLICIES TOWARDS INDIGENOUS PEOPLES

Political and Military Policies

> Our plans at present are to use native princes as the instru-
> ments of military government, according to their former
> status and ability.

The above-mentioned statement featured as the first priority
in the three-point strategy for the development of North
Borneo which allowed the native elite to fill positions vacated
by their former European masters in positions of authority,
generally subjected to Japanese supervision. Undoubtedly the
Japanese intention was to win the support of the indigenous
peoples through the influence of their leaders.

A good example of utilizing 'native princes as the instruments of military government' was the creation of the *Ken Sanjikai*, or Prefectural Advisory District Councils, in each provincial centre. The establishment of these councils was in accordance with a military decree issued on 1 October 1943.[18] Each council comprised between five and ten Malay and Iban community leaders, each individually appointed by the Governor of the Province acting upon the recommendation of the Japanese District Chief. In Kuching, Abang Haji Suleiman and Abang Haji Mustapha (the *Datu Amar* and *Datu Pahlawan* respectively), Haji Abdul Rahman, a noted intellectual and religious scholar, and Native Officers Abang Openg and Tuanku Bujang were appointed as *ken-sanji*. The Iban appointees were Charles Mason and Philip Jitam, both regarded as the unofficial leaders of the Iban community in Kuching by virtue of their position as the most senior Iban government employees in the district. In Sibu, Jugah anak Barieng was elevated to the status of a *ken-sanji* owing to his position as a *Penghulu* (a headman).[19]

The *ken-sanji* were instructed to hold bi-annual meetings under the chairmanship of the Japanese District Chief. It is unclear exactly how the *Ken Sanjikai* served the military authorities in its capacity as an advisory council. In Kuching, its members were instructed 'to assist with the various economic projects which had been planned, including a shipyard to make wooden hulls from local timber and a factory to extract oil from rubber latex'.[20] In the case of Jugah, his status as a *ken-sanji* was ambivalent, although there was no doubt that he was much feared by the people as the following recollections by a contemporary indicate:

> We didn't know what *sanji* meant, didn't know how to interpret it. It's Japanese for some sort of position ... I don't know what Jugah did as a *sanji*, but just as people were fearful of the Japanese, it carried over to him. [In those days] if we did something wrong, and some one like Jugah found out about it, he couldn't punish us, but they [the Japanese] could. So everyone was afraid of him. If people talked with him, they watched what they said.[21]

The *ken-sanji*, being community leaders, were expected to solicit popular support from the masses for the Japanese cause by giving speeches and talks during public gatherings and official functions. Both Abang Haji Mustapha and Jugah were known to have been speakers at Japanese-organized public functions. Abang Haji Mustapha had been accused of giving pro-Japanese speeches at public gatherings.[22] But for Jugah, his wit and usage of words made his speeches noncommittal to either his Japanese masters or to the Allied cause. An observer of one of his public addresses in Sibu during those days recalled the event:

> He was so cunning, and said, 'We did not have this kind of entertainment before the Japanese.' He made his speech in such a way that you couldn't say he was anti-Japanese or anti-British. He was getting his digs in, but in a very clever way. He said, 'If you had come to a show like this before the Japanese came, you would have had to pay.'[23]

However, a clearer manifestation of the policy of using indigenous leaders 'as the instruments of military government' was the emplacement of the educated Iban elite in positions of authority in the largely Iban populated districts of the Lupar and Saribas river systems, namely the Second Division. As early as January 1942, the Japanese authorities appointed Eliab Bay as Liaison Officer for the Second Division, in effect becoming the Resident of that Division, a position that was reserved exclusively for an European officer during Brooke days.[24] The mission-educated Bay, who was a court writer at Simanggang prior to the occupation, was selected by the Japanese as their valuable 'instrument' owing to his position as the most senior Iban clerk of the Second Division.[25] On Bay's recommendation, the Japanese assigned other Ibans to positions of authority such as *guncho* (District Officer), hitherto held by only Europeans under the Brookes. In his newly elevated post, Bay recommended other Ibans to positions of authority, including DOs who were in large measure responsible to him.

By using Bay and other educated Ibans in the day-to-day administration of the whole Second Division, the Japanese military authorities succeeded in attaining the proverbial goal of 'killing two birds with one stone': it overcame the Japanese lack of personnel, particularly civil administrators, and at the same time utilized the Iban educated elite in governing a largely Iban inhabited province, which reduced the difficulties relating to direct rule by a foreign regime. In the eyes of the majority of the Iban people of the Second Division, Bay and his compatriots were seen as 'Native Officers' of the new regime, not so very different from the previous government, except that they wielded more power in the absence of the 'White Tuan'.

The Japanese also utilized this system of indirect rule in other parts of the country whereby the majority of Malay and Iban civil servants and police personnel were retained in their posts. The following situation in Lawas and Trusan is typical of other districts as well:

> In government ... the Lawas-Trusan area received no Japanese replacements for officials; instead the administrative staff in Lawas town remained the same, consisting of Acting D[istrict] O[fficer] Adenan and assisted by N[ative] O[fficer] Bugar[,] [t]he Chief Clerk, Mr. Hugo Low, and five other clerks. To the local police only one or two new men were added, in each case the newcomer was a Malay from Brunei. All the local officials were responsible to their [Japanese] superior officers stationed in Brunei which had become the Japanese administrative centre for the Brunei Bay territory.[26]

Administration in most of the outlying districts and the interior was left in the hands of native police personnel and village headmen.

The Japanese authorities attempted to tap the labour resources of the indigenous population for military purposes. Several examples whereby native workmen were conscripted to build and/or repair military installations, such as airfields, were reported. For instance, the construction of the Bintulu landing ground utilized forced native labour recruited from the surrounding districts. 'Each longhouse in the Bintulu area', a contemporary recalled, 'was required in turn to send all adult males to work for one month. The work was hard and the supplies meagre.'[27] The workers were required to bring their own food and were paid in kerosene and sugar. The construction of the Labuan airstrip relied on indigenous labour from the Lawas-Trusan basins.[28] Besides the obvious objective of such work, it has also been suggested that 'the JAPANESE intention was to degrade the natives to coolie status, unless the KYODOTAI and other organizations were successful in making them more or less willing tools'.[29]

The North Borneo Volunteer Corps (or *kyodotai*) was constituted on 10 October 1943 with recruitment limited to 'all native inhabitants of BRITISH BORNEO', namely, 'DUSUNS, MALAYS, BAJANS [BAJAUS], SEA DYAKS, LAND DYAKS AND MARUTS [MURUTS]'.[30] Even before October 1943, there was already recruitment of native men grouped into small units for military training; these units were subsequently incorporated in the *kyodotai*. The *kyodotai* aimed

> to train future village chiefs to accept the JAPANESE occupation, absorb JAPANESE ideals and ideas and work in harmony with the JAPANESE. After a two year course, trainees were to be returned to their kampongs [villages] as headmen, when they would be in a position to inculcate [pass] what they themselves had learned on [to] their villagers.[31]

Volunteers were expected to submit applications to join as trainees. Only candidates that were deemed to be 'sufficiently intelligent to be able to absorb the doctrines' were considered.[32] The Japanese Governor of each province would review applications submitted by prospective candidates, scrutinize their background, and recommend their acceptance or rejection as trainees. Overall, 830 men were recruited as trainees: 350 to the Kuching Company, 300 to the Sibu Company, and 180 to the Miri Company.[33]

The two-year training programme was divided into two parts: a six-month basic training course in military subjects ('drill, use of arms, aircraft recognition, infantry tactics and defence position training') and the teaching of the 'three Rs', with the remaining eighteen months devoted to 'specialist training in farming, building, sanitation, hygiene, field works and engineering and ... understanding of communication'.[34] Throughout the two years of training, trainees were also instructed in the Japanese language, and Japanese imperial history and geography.

Another *Gunseibu*-sponsored organization which sought to make use of natives for military purposes was a kind of vigilante corps or auxiliary police, an organization not unlike the *jikeidan* set-up in Malaya.[35] The *jikeidan* system, as practised in Sarawak, is structured as follows:

> A leader is appointed for every group of ten households and a superior for every group of 30 households, 100 households, and so on. Householders are detailed to patrol the streets at night, to enforce blackout and other forms of A.R.P. [Air Raid Precaution] and to question strangers or suspects.[36]

In the upriver districts the longhouse constituted the *jikeidan* unit with the *tuai rumah* (headman) as the leader. The *jikeidan*, for all intents and purposes, acted as a security force which the Japanese military intelligence utilized to counter any anti-Japanese and subversive tendencies among the populace.

Malays and Ibans were known to have been employed by the Japanese authorities to serve as naval ratings wearing an 'anchor insignia surrounded by a laurel wreath in red on the left arm and on their cloth caps'.[37] Their assignments complemented the work of the marine branch of the *Kempeitai* (Japanese Military Police) which was responsible for enforcing counter-intelligence measures in the coastal districts where they maintained tight security over ports and jetties.

Besides retaining the majority of police personnel, the Japanese also launched a drive for new recruits, particularly among Malays and Ibans.[38] Several Ibans who joined the police force prior to the invasion gained rapid promotion to 'positions of considerable responsibility',[39] while 'A Malay sub-inspector was appointed to command the Police force at Kuching.'[40]

In an attempt to garner native support, the Japanese contributed a sum of $4000.00[41] towards the funding of a native organization, the Perimpun Dayak. The Perimpun Dayak, an Iban-based pro-Japanese political organization, had beginnings in the pre-war Dayaks Co-operative Society, whence it drew the bulk of its membership.[42] The aim of the Perimpun Dayak was the promotion of Iban loyalty to the Japanese regime. This objective could be clearly seen in the programme prepared for its inaugural meeting in Kuching on 17 February 1944. Among other things, it listed the following instructions that members had to abide by.

   i. Fall-in in the play-ground at the back of the school (Maderasah Melayu)

  ii. Give respect due to H.I.M. [His Imperial Majesty] the Emperor of Japan. Facing east: *Kiojo yo hai* 'SAIKEREI' body bending 45 degrees, silence for 1/2 minute – *Naure* –

 iii. Give respect due to the noble and brave heroes of the Nipponese soldiers who sacrificed their lives for the sake of Dai Toa at the fronts: *Nippon Gun ni tai suru Kansha no Mokuto hajime* – 1 minute silence head bending, eyes shut.[43]

The Japanese supported its work in conducting a census of the population of the Ibans and Land Dayaks of the First and Second Divisions, but it was unclear to what purpose and to what extent its findings were used by the Japanese. The Perimpun Dayak was the organizing body for cultural items such as Iban dances which were staged during ceremonial functions.

Economic Policies: Oil Production, Food Self-Sufficiency and Timber Output

> We must maintain the use of a part of the local vital resources, particularly oil, as reserve stocks.

Despite the denial schemes and scorched earth tactics employed to render the oil fields at Miri and the refinery at Lutong useless to the enemy, the Japanese had succeeded in reviving oil production almost to pre-war capacity by late 1944. Allied aerial reconnaissance photographs showed that the Japanese managed to acquire most of the pumping equipment which had been shipped to Singapore during the weeks prior to invasion. Furthermore, photographic evidence revealed the availability of new equipment. It was estimated that the Japanese managed to produce 1200 barrels per day throughout 1944.[44] Restoration of the Lutong refinery was impressive. Photographs taken in October 1944

> revealed the Japanese facilities as fourteen tanks with a total capacity of 600 000 barrels ... approximately equal to the pre-war capacity of 650 000 barrels. Photographs also showed that there was sufficient pipe available for three completely new lines three miles long ... It is quite evident however, that the lines had been repaired by the Japanese for almost 11 000 000 barrels of crude and fuel oil as well as approximately 4 600 000 barrels of finished refinery products [which] were shipped from the area in the period July 1, 1943, to June 30, 1944.[45]

It was clear that the Japanese managed to revive the Miri oil fields and the Lutong refinery to produce fuel resources vital to Japan's wartime economy.

The objective of self-sufficiency in food production was at the forefront of the economic policy of the Japanese. According to the general policy for the administration of occupied territories, three main points were emphasized, listed as follows according to their order of importance:

(a) maintaining of law and order;
(b) developing and increasing production of raw materials and generally exploiting of natural wealth;
(c) making each area self-sufficient.[46]

However, as the tide of war turned against Japan from mid-1944 with the increased frequency of Allied bombings on

Japan's sea links with her Southern Area (South-East Asia),
self-sufficiency became the main priority. The campaign for
increasing local food production involved the direct participation of the various native communities which hitherto had
been largely subsistence-based in orientation. Two agricultural programmes aimed at stimulating the cultivation of food
crops were initiated in *Kuching-shu*, namely, government-
managed agricultural stations, and government subsidized
settlement schemes ('agricultural concentrations').[47]

The concept of establishing government agricultural stations had been in practice since the days of James Brooke.[48]
By the time of the Japanese invasion, the only government-
run farm was the Central Agricultural Station at Semenggok
which continued to function until its closure in late 1942.
Earlier, in March 1942, the Japanese opened a new
Agricultural Training Centre at Tarat, located at the 34th
Mile, Simanggang Road. The Tarat Centre 'comprised about
40 hectares of gently undulating, relatively fertile land and
was used as a demonstration farm for the cultivation of a
range of food crops'.[49] A farm school was also established at
Tarat offering a three-month course including Japanese language instruction.[50] In April 1944, the Sekama Vegetable
Garden was opened for the cultivation of various vegetable
crops to supply the Japanese administration in Kuching. In
the outstations, similar large-sized vegetable gardens were
established: for instance, 'one just above Lawas town, another
a little above Trusan bazaar and a third on the Merapok
River'.[51]

The concept of government-subsidized settlement schemes
was not a Japanese import but had precedents in the 1930s
when several agricultural (*padi*) settlement schemes were initiated.[52] The Japanese military authorities organized similar
government-subsidized settlement schemes along these lines:

> The [Japanese] administration would select a suitable area
> and demarcate it into lots. It would then select a leader
> who undertook to recruit other settlers. The settlers were
> required to plant specified food crops, such as rice, sweet

potato and maize. The settlers erected their own houses with timber and materials supplied free of charge by the administration. Tools, rations and cash advances of up to $18 per person per month were supplied for a maximum of one year. These were treated as loans, to be repaid in instalments through the sale of produce to the administration. The administration guaranteed to buy all the produce from the concentration at prices which were fixed in advance by agreement. The leader was held accountable for all loans advanced to his settlers and had to provide security in the form of land titles or other assets. He also had to keep a record of all transactions relating to the concentration. In return he received 25 per cent of the concentration's earnings. The administration also undertook to indemnify him against any losses due to factors beyond his control. Termination of the agreement between the administration and the leaders required eight months' notice on either side.[53]

It was estimated that 1000 hectares (2470 acres) along the Simanggang Road were converted into 'agricultural concentrations'.[54] The wet-rice scheme at Bijat in the Second Division, which was initiated before the war, was completed and achieved remarkable results under the supervision of Eliab Bay, the Iban Liaison Officer based at Simanggang.[55]

Elsewhere, in most parts of the country, the Japanese strongly encouraged farmers to increase food crop production. Coercion was used where efforts appeared wanting.[56]

The Japanese military authorities, as part of the overall strategy of increasing food production, appointed agents in each province to purchase foodcrops at controlled prices for consumption by the soldiers and the urban population. Mitsui, a Japanese *zaibatsu*, operated through its trading arm, Mitsui Bussan, the monopoly agency for the purchase and distribution of all foodstuffs in *Kuching-shu*.[57] In Lawas town a local Chinese consortium, Soon Teck Kongsi, acted as agent for the entire Lawas district. Soon Teck Kongsi was, in fact, a Japanese 'creation' that was set up in early 1942 when two major Chinese shops in the bazaar, Guan Soon and Hoon Teck, were instructed to combine.[58]

Besides the promotion of increasing the output of food crops, the Japanese military government was also keen to exploit the timber resources of the Sarawak rainforest. The interest shown in tapping timber resources was in line with the expressed basic policy of economic administration expounded by the Japanese Navy National Research Committee (April 1939). Included in the nine-point objective of promoting industries in the regions under Japanese guidance is the following statement regarding Borneo (Sarawak):

> to develop undeveloped areas such as New Guinea, Mindanao, Borneo, etc.; At the same time to promote utilization and development of forests in the Philippines, Borneo, Celebes, New Guinea, etc.[59]

The building of launches and small craft for the transportation of goods to and from large Japanese ships anchoring off the coast was the main concern in acquiring large amounts of timber. The Japanese operated logging camps on the Leba'an in the Rejang delta and in the Lassa River near Bawang Assan downriver from Sibu town; a timber collection centre was established at Seputin near Kapit.[60] Chinese-owned sawmills in Bintulu and Sibu and elsewhere were commandeered to produce sawn timber for military purposes like shipbuilding and for the repairs in the oil fields.[61] According to a contemporary account the sawmills at Bintulu produced some 4000 tons of sawn timber.[62] In all these operations, natives supplied the bulk of the work force by serving in logging camps and working sawmills.

Socio-Cultural Policies

> In Lawas town everyone went to school for two hours a day to learn the Japanese language. Three teachers, one local Chinese, a local Malay and one Brunei Malay, were trained in Brunei to teach all of the local people this new tongue. Every morning the Lawas school children assembled to

sing the Japanese National Anthem as the flag of the
Rising Sun went up the school flagpole. During the day any
Japanese officer or soldiers who visited were greeted by the
local people with a deep ninety degree bow and were called
'Tuan' [Sir]. Failure to follow these rules of respect would
result in a sharp slap from the Japanese present.[63]

The socio-cultural policy of the Japanese military regime
towards indigenous peoples was to inculcate anti-European
feelings and attitudes, replacing them with pro-Japanese sentiments and loyalties. The propaganda section of the administration churned out materials in both Malay and the Iban
language which extolled the benefits and virtues of the
'Greater East Asia Co-Prosperity Sphere' and 'Asia for
Asians' concepts. Community leaders were invited to give
speeches at public gatherings to promote the Japanese cause,
and at the same time to denounce the Allied powers. Some
Malay leaders spoke scathingly against America and Britain
at Japanese-sponsored *kampong* loyalty meetings.

The promotion of Japanese-language learning was initiated
in larger towns such as Kuching, Sibu and Miri, where Malay
and Chinese schools remained open for this purpose. In the
outlying districts, school houses became centres for *Nippon-
go* instruction to local children and adults. Young Malay
and Chinese adults attended *Nippon-go* classes to train as
interpreters.[64]

In addition to language instruction, school children were
taught Japanese moral values, discipline, state ideology
(emperor worship), Japanese imperial history and the geography of the Japanese islands. Physical training, the singing
of the Japanese national anthem and rituals connected with
emperor worship were incorporated in the daily curriculum.

'Cultural shows', featuring school children singing Japanese
songs and performing for the entertainment of Japanese
officers and local people, were staged as a public relations
exercise aimed at improving relations between the Japanese
authorities and their newly conquered subjects. It was during
such public gatherings that native community leaders were

urged to give pro-Japanese speeches to win over their countrymen.

The Japanese also tried to promote thriftiness among the Ibans with visits to upriver longhouses in the Rejang 'to get the people to *simpan duit* (save money)'.[65] Little is known, however, about whether such visits occurred in other upriver areas.

In line with the general policy of 'conciliating the Muslims in the Southern Area',[66] the *Gunseibu* courted the local Muslim populace, namely Malays and Melanaus, to garner their support for the Japanese cause.

JAPANESE ATTITUDES TOWARDS THE CHINESE

The political power of local Chinese must be restricted as soon as possible.

As the Chinese in Sarawak were generally politically inert, the Japanese authorities did not have to resort to stern measures to clamp down on suspected subversive activities. There were no incidents of mass executions of Chinese, and certainly nothing comparable to the situation in neighbouring Singapore and Malaya.[67]

However, at Jesselton, in neighbouring former British North Borneo, a Chinese-led anti-Japanese revolt broke out. A combined force of Chinese and Bajaus staged an uprising on 10 October 1943, 'The Double Tenth'. All the Japanese, about fifty altogether, stationed between Jesselton and Tuaran were killed. The town of Jesselton was 'liberated'. The Japanese counter-offensive was swift and merciless. Coastal settlements were bombed and strafed with machine-gun fire, whole villages were burnt and hundreds of people were interrogated and tortured to death. Jesselton was re-occupied. On 19 December, Albert Kwok Fen Nam, the leader of the revolt, surrendered. He and 175 others were executed on 21 January 1944 at Petagas; another 131 were imprisoned at Labuan 'where all but nine died before the liberation'.[68]

It was only after this 'Double Tenth' uprising and the American capture of Morotai in the Halmaheras in mid-1944 which enabled the bombing of shipping in the Brunei Bay area, that the Japanese became more vigilant regarding the local inhabitants as the tide of war begun to turn against them. Nevertheless, even after the Jesselton uprising, surprisingly there were no witch-hunts among the Chinese community in Sarawak.

The majority of Sarawak Chinese resorted to non-cooperation by avoiding contact with the occupying forces. A considerable number of Chinese from the urban areas and the main river ports moved to the coastal districts, to the interior or to less accessible areas in their attempt to avoid contact with the Japanese lest they be forced to cooperate with the new regime. It was estimated that 'at least 30 per cent and possibly as many as 50 or 60 per cent of the Chinese' inhabitants of Kuching migrated to the coastal and interior areas of the First and Second Divisions.[69] They avoided being forced into labour contingents which the Japanese utilized for work at military installations like the repair of the landing ground at Kuching or in the construction of the Labuan aerodrome. The Japanese had to rely on imported forced labourers from abroad, like Javanese and Shanghainese, for their construction work owing to the difficulty in procuring local workers.[70] POWs and civilian male internees from Batu Lintang Camp were pressed into work at the Bukit Stabar landing ground, and as stevedores at the Kuching harbour.[71] For the women, escape into the countryside meant the hope of avoiding rape by the Japanese. Many Chinese women of marriageable age were hastily married off to avoid being sent to brothels.[72] This urban-rural migration of the Chinese was also a practical move, enabling them to engage in subsistence farming at a time when food shortages were developing in the towns, which had always depended on imports.[73]

Those Chinese who remained in the towns had to serve the Japanese or face punishment and imprisonment. The majority cooperated with the Japanese reluctantly, but some individuals seized the opportunity offered by wartime conditions to benefit economically by enthusiastically collaborating with the invaders.

Monetary contribution was exacted from the Chinese community as a form of *sook ching* (cleansing or purification through deeds) for their support of China in the war against Japan. The Overseas Chinese Association was entrusted with the task of collecting forced donations amounting to $2 million allocated as follows: $900 000 for Kuching, $700 000 for Sibu, and $300 000 for Miri; and North Borneo was expected to contribute $1.2 million.[74]

'GUESTS' OF HIS IMPERIAL MAJESTY THE EMPEROR OF JAPAN

The entire European population of Sarawak, and those of British North Borneo, were interned behind barbed wire fencing throughout the occupation. The Imperial Japanese forces headquarters for all civilian and POW internment camps was located at Batu Lintang, to the south-west of Kuching town. The Batu Lintang Camp, formerly the premises of the barracks of the 2nd/15th Punjab Regiment, housed both civilian internees and POWs. The entire camp was enclosed within a five-mile barbed wire fence. The internees were segregated under various categories into wired-in compounds as follows: Australian officers and non-commissioned officers (NCOs); Dutch and Indonesians; British officers; British other ranks; civilian male internees; women and children internees; Dutch Roman Catholic priests; and, Indian Army (2nd/15th Punjab Regiment). British officers and their men were initially confined within the same compound. However, from 5 February 1943, the officers were removed to another compound presumably for fear of subversive activities. The remnants of the 2nd/15th Punjab Regiment were brought to Batu Lintang after their capitulation.

The segregation pattern and security features of Batu Lintang, in the words of a former inmate, were as follows:

> Groups of huts were separated into 'Compounds' by barbed-wire aproned fencing, and the whole 'Compound' area was encircled by double fencing between which ran a path. Along this path, at strategic intervals, were watch towers with a guard in each, and the whole path was patrolled. An outer perimeter fence enclosed the whole Camp area, the land between the outer and inner perimeter fences being, at a later stage, cleared and cultivated.[75]

At the apex of the command structure in Batu Lintang was Major (later Lieutenant-Colonel) Tatsuji Suga, who was the Camp Commandant of all POW and internment facilities throughout North Borneo. Smaller internment camps operated in Jesselton, Sandakan and for a brief period in Labuan. Being overall commandant, Suga was often called away. The next senior officer at Batu Lintang was Lieutenant (later Captain) Nekata, who assumed control in the absence of Suga. Lieutenant Ogema also played an important role in camp administration. Lieutenant 'Doctor' Yamamoto, presumably a medical practitioner, served as the camp's medical officer. The Quartermaster was Lieutenant Takino. Lieutenant Watanabe was an officer who dealt mostly with the administrative and other bureaucratic matters of the camp. Most of the rank and file constituting the camp guards were Koreans, with a few Formosans.

Prior to their transfer to the main camp at Batu Lintang, many internees upon their surrender and/or capture by the Japanese spent brief periods at transit or temporary camps. A series of rules and regulations, and the numerous restrictions and prohibitions, dictated the daily existence of internees; not surprisingly, all these regulations and prohibitions were strictly enforced in the compounds of POWs.[76]

Comparatively the POWs were treated much more severely by the Japanese. For obvious reasons, they were under greater surveillance and suspicion *vis-à-vis* their civilian counterparts. Harsh punishments were meted out on a much more regular basis; slappings and, not infrequently, severe beatings, were common for minor infractions of camp regulations. The *Kempeitai* were called in for serious intransigence or suspected subversive activities. Those who survived a *Kempeitai* encounter often returned after being beaten senseless; some, however, were not seen again.

The POWs and male civilian internees, as mentioned earlier, were employed in the reconstruction of the Bukit Stabar landing grounds. These 'White coolies' led a life of drudgery and continuous hard labour, interrupted only by beatings or sickness, whether they toiled the entire day in the sun at the 7th Milestone airstrip or performing stevedore work at the Kuching harbour. During the later part of the war years when the food situation became critical, their labour was also utilized to produce foodstuff; accordingly, land around the camp was cleared for cultivation.

The female internees were given less strenuous tasks such as laundry, cooking, cleaning, sewing and repairing clothing and other domestic chores, whereas outdoors, they had to do gardening, growing food crops and vegetables to supplement the kitchen. Women with young children had a far harder time as they had to take care of and fend for their children under trying situations of food shortages, and the childeren were more susceptible to the widespread illnesses than the adults. Women and children were generally spared the wrath of the camp guards, and Japanese officers were surprisingly restrained and disciplined when dealing with this group of internees.

CONCLUSION

For three years and eight months Sarawak was a part of the extensive Japanese Imperial Empire. The Japanese campaign of an 'Asia for Asians' and the attempted realization of 'The Greater East Asia Co-Prosperity Sphere' were both played out on the Sarawak stage. The *Gunseibu* implemented policies, formulated by Tokyo planners, which encompassed political, military, economic and socio-cultural fields. As pointed out, the Japanese achieved an unqualified success in the revitalization of the oil fields and oil production. On the other hand, indigenous and Chinese participation in Japanese-sponsored organizations and the consequent effects, and to what extent the avowed objectives of wartime policies were attained, will be the focus of discussion in the following chapters.

Notes

1. At mid-day on 19 December 1941 Kuching experienced its first air raid when fifteen to seventeen Japanese planes bombed the town and the landing ground at the 7th Mile. The number of casualties was uncertain (estimates ranged from eighty to 100), but all reportedly were civilians. Mukah and Sibu were also bombed on 23 and 25 December respectively with civilian casualties reported. See K. D. Shargava and K. N. V. Sastri, *Official History of the Indian Armed Forces in the Second World War, 1939–45: Campaigns in South-East Asia, 1941–42* (Combined Inter-Services Historical Section India and Pakistan: City Orient Longmans, 1960) pp. 376–7; Leonard Edwards and Peter W. Stevens, *Short Histories of the Lawas and Kanowit Districts* (Kuching: Borneo Literature Bureau, 1971) p. 161; and 'The Japanese Occupation: Extracts from a broadcast interview with Tan Sri Ong Kee Hui by Christopher Chan on 14 February 1975', *Journal of the Malaysian Historical Society (JMHSSB)*, 3 (December 1976) 4.
2. 'The Administration of the Occupied Territories in the Vital Southern Area', Special Intelligence Bulletin: Japanese Plans and Operation in S.E. Asia – Translation of Japanese Documents, 21 December 1945 (W0 203/6310, PRO) Document 3.
3. Ibid.
4. See 'Special Intelligence Bulletin: Japanese Plans and Operations in S.E. Asia – Translation of Japanese Documents, 21 Dec. 1945. Document 4: "Army-Navy-Central Agreement for establishing Military Administration in Occupied Territories"' (WO 203/6310, PRO) p. 6.
   In late 1943 the headquarters was removed to Jesselton which was better positioned to face of an Allied invasion. Also, the timing of the transfer in late 1943 coincided with the clampdown on the Chinese uprising in Jesselton of October.

See below. Dutch Borneo, on the other hand, was administered separately by the Japanese Navy.

5. A post-war Australian document dated September 1945 lists
the principal Japanese administrators in British Borneo as
follows:

General Masataka YAMAWAKI	Commander-in-Chief, Japanese Expeditionary Forces in Borneo
Taneki KUNABE	Governor, East Coast State (BNB)
Yoshimasa MURAKAMI	Governor, West Coast State (BNB)
Roichi KODAMA	Governor, Miri State (Brunei and N. Sarawak)
Sotojiro TOKUNO	Governor, Kuching State (Sarawak)

'British Territories in North Borneo', extract from Allied
Land Forces South-East Asia, No.52, 28 September 1945
(WO 208/105 PRO) p. 23.

Interestingly there is no reference to *Sibu-shu* in the above
paper although in other documents there was mention of an
administrative prefecture in existence in the Rejang with Sibu
as its centre. See 'Interrogation Report No. 21: Interrogation
of Saburoo KAWADA, Senior Administrative Official in the
Civil Administration, 4 Mar. 1946' (WO 208/3114, PRO) p. 1;
and 'Intelligence Bulletin No. 237, Item 2178: Interrogation
of Manabu KUJI, Governor of West Coast (Jesselton) Province
(20 Nov. 1943–1 Jun. 1945), North Borneo; Subject: Japanese
Civil Administration in British North Borneo; c. mid-1946'
(WO 203/6317, PRO) p. 1.

Sibu-shu might be a minor prefecture under the control of
senior administrative officers. On the other hand, its omission
from Australian documents suggests that such a prefecture
possibly did exist but after the transfer of the 37th Army headquarters to Jesselton in the aftermath of the Chinese insurrection of October 1943, it was thought expedient to reduce
the number of administrative units in Sarawak territory
thereby allowing more focus on North Borneo. Sarawak, after
all, appeared to be a relatively trouble-free zone.

6. According to one account, Dutch submarines torpedoed the
four transports off Kuching while another source maintains
that they were sunk by Dutch aircraft. See Lionel Wigmore,
The Japanese Thrust (Canberra: Australian War Memorial,

1957) p. 180, and R. H. W. Reece, *The Name of Brooke: The End of White Rajah Rule in Sarawak* (Kuala Lumpur: Oxford University Press, 1982) p. 143.

7.   See Edwards and Stevens, *Lawas and Kanowit*, pp. 49–50, 51, 161–2.

8.   See Vinson H. Sutlive, Jr, *Tun Jugah of Sarawak: Colonialism and Iban Response* (Kuala Lumpur: Penerbit Fajar Bakti for Sarawak Literary Society, 1992) pp. 102–3.

9.   For the workings of the Council in Kuching, see Reece, *Name of Brooke*, p. 144.

10. 'British Territories in North Borneo', p. 22.

11. 'Intelligence Bulletin No. 237, Item 2182: Interrogation of Lieutenants Yoshihiko WAKAMATSU and Kenzo MORIKAWA, and Captains Ryuji IKENO, Minoru TASUMA and Yoshio WATANABE, all officers attached to the North Borneo Volunteer Corps (KYODOTAI); Subject: North Borneo Volunteer Corps; c. mid-1946' (WO 203/6317, PRO) p. 12. However, John M. Chin states that young Chinese men 'disappeared' into the rural areas 'to avoid being recruited into the *kyodo-hei* [*kyodotai*]'. This was, however, unlikely to be the case. See John M. Chin, *The Sarawak Chinese* (Kuala Lumpur: Oxford University Press, 1981) p. 98.

12. 'British Territories in North Borneo', p. 23.

13. See C. A. Lockard, 'The Southeast Asian Town in Historical Perspective: A Social History of Kuching, Malaysia, 1820–1970' (Ph.D. thesis, University of Wisconsin, 1973) II, p. 459; and Edwards and Stevens, *Lawas and Kanowit*, p. 53.

14. See *Sarawak Tribune (ST)*, 19 January 1946 and *ST*, 21 February 1950.

15. *ST*, 13 December 1970.

16. See Reece, *Name of Brooke*, p. 144.

17. 'Special Intelligence Bulletin: Japanese Plans and Operations in S.E. Asia – Translation of Japanese Documents, 21 Dec. 1945. Document 11: "Summary of the government of occupied territory in the Southern Area, 12 Oct. [19]42"' (W0 203/6310, PRO) p. 24.

18. Extract of Tokyo broadcast dated 1 October 1943, Sarawak Government Agency, Sydney, Circular No.5/43, 12 October 1943, cited by Reece, *Name of Brooke*, p. 144.

19. See Sutlive, *Tun Jugah*, p. 104.

20. Reece, *Name of Brooke*, p. 144.

21. Sng Chin Joo, interview, Meligai Hotel, Kapit, 1 August 1987, cited in Sutlive, *Tun Jugah*, p. 104.

22. See Joseph Law to Bertram Brooke, 31 May 1946, Brooke Papers (MSS Pac. s. 83, Box 2/3, RHL); 'Statement by Mohd.

Ma'amon bin Nor', 29 July 1946 Brooke Papers (MSS Pac. s. 83, Box 22, RHL); and K. H. Digby, *Lawyer in the Wilderness*, p. 173.

23.   Harry Buxton, interview, Aurora Coffee Shop, Kuching, 12 July 1988, cited in Sutlive, *Tun Jugah*, p. 107.

24.   K. Itoh to Datu Abang Zin Gapor, 9 January 1942, Eliab Bay Papers, cited in Reece, *Name of Brooke*, p. 147.

25.   Bay had held various government posts in the Second Division including court writer at Engkilili, Sebuyau, Lingga and Lubok Antu, and as Treasury clerk and store keeper at Simanggang, prior to his appointment as court writer at Simanggang, the headquarters of the Division. He had also attempted to champion the rights of the Asiatic members of the Brooke Junior Service. For his biographical background and career prior to the war, see Reece, *Name of Brooke*, pp. 138–41.

26.   Edwards and Stevens, *Lawas and Kanowit*, p. 51. See also Lockard, 'Kuching' II, pp. 460–1.

27.   Quoting Harry Buxton, a Brooke Forestry Officer during the 1930s, who was a prisoner of the Japanese at Bintulu during the occupation. Sutlive, *Tun Jugah*, p. 107. Although citing Buxton as his source, Reece stated that the Ibans would work for two weeks at a time. See Reece, *Name of Brooke*, p. 149.

28.   See Chong Ah Onn, '1943–46, Fifth Division, Sarawak – Pt. II', *SG*, 31 December 1952, p. 283.

29.   'Intelligence Bulletin No. 237, Item 2184: Interrogation of Major General Shigeru KURODA, 37th Army HQ; Subject: 12. Japanese Policy in Far East' (WO 203/6317, PRO) p. 31.

30.   'KYODOTAI', p. 12.

31.   Ibid.

32.   Ibid.

33.   In former British North Borneo, 450 natives were accepted into the *kyodotai*; 300 in the Keningau Company, and 150 in the Sandakan Company. Ibid.

34.   Ibid.

35.   The *jikeidan* organizations established in Perak, Penang, Malacca and Selangor, and presumably also in other parts of Malaya, were adjuncts to the state and military police forces. The system was organized such that a group of households was made collectively responsible for any anti-social, and in particular, subversive activities. See Cheah Boon Kheng, 'The Social Impact of the Japanese Occupation of Malaya (1942–1945)', in *Southeast Asia Under Japanese Occupation*, ed. Alfred W. McCoy (Monograph Series No. 22, Yale University Southeast Asia Studies, New Haven: Yale University Southeast Asia Studies, 1980) p. 103.

36. 'British Territories in North Borneo', p. 23.
37. Ibid.
38. Chinese were also recruited into the police force from mid-1944 for services in Chinese populated areas like in the Lower Rejang districts. See ibid. Apparently such a policy was aimed at stamping out subversive activities in Chinese settlements as Chinese constables would be in a better position to overcome the language barrier than their native counterpart. Although there were no incidents in Sarawak similar to the October 1943 Chinese-led revolt in Jesselton, it was no doubt part of a Japanese concerted effort to prevent such a recurrence.
39. Reece, *Name of Brooke*, p. 147.
40. 'British Territories in North Borneo', p. 23.
41. Unless stated otherwise, all currencies refer to the Sarawak dollar which was tied to the Straits Settlements dollar, and tended to fluctuate in value. From 1906 the Straits Dollar was pegged to Sterling at the rate of $1 to 2*s* 4*d*., or $8.57 to £1, which was generally maintained.
42. The leadership of the Perimpun was from the educated Iban elite; Charles Mason and Philip Jitam, who both served as *ken-sanji*, were its president and secretary respectively. See Reece, *Name of Brooke*, pp. 138, 145.
43. Programme of inaugural meeting of Perimpun Dayak, Papers of Philip Jitam, cited by Reece, *Name of Brooke*, p. 145.
44. See 'Borneo: Oilfields, 19 September 1945' (WO208/104, PRO) p. 6.
45. Ibid., p. 7.
46. 'Japanese Civil Administration', p. 2.
47. R. A Cramb, 'The Impact of the Japanese Occupation on Agricultural Development in Sarawak', 1994/1995, MS (Personal Copy), p. 15.
48. The idea of establishing an agricultural farm to instruct natives in Western/modern methods of farming and the planting of new crops was started by Miss (later Baroness) Angela Burdett Coutts, a friend and benefactor of James Brooke, during the mid-1860s. Although Coutts's Quop Estate was unsuccessful, Charles Brooke, the Second Rajah, incorporated the concept of the government-managed experimental farm in his agricultural programme, and several such farms were initiated in Kuching and in the outstations. Rajah Vyner continued his predecessor's agricultural programme. See Ooi Keat Gin, *Of Free Trade and Native Interests: The Brookes and the Economic Development of Sarawak, 1841–1941* (Kuala Lumpur: Oxford University Press, 1997) pp. 165–98.
49. Cramb, 'Agricultural Development', p. 15.
50. Ibid., pp. 15–16.

51. Edwards and Stevens, *Lawas and Kanowit*, p. 54.
52. The concept of designating areas of *padi* reserves and establishing *padi* farming communities of Chinese, Javanese, Japanese and Bugis, was implemented during the 1930s. See *SAR 1929*, p. 22; *SG*, 1 November 1930, p. 279; *SG*, 2 January 1931, p. 11; *SG*, 1 April 1931, p. 83; *SAR 1931*, p. 8; *SG*, 1 January 1932, p. 8; *SG*, 1 July 1932, p. 126; *SG*, 1 November 1933, p. 144; *SG*, 2 January 1936, p. 16; and 1 April 1936, p. 87.
53. Ong Kee Hui, *Report on the Department of Agriculture, Sarawak, June 1941–June 1945* (Kuching, 1945), cited in Cramb, 'Agricultural Development', pp. 16–17.
54. Cramb, 'Agricultural Development', p. 17.
55. See Reece, *Name of Brooke*, pp. 147, 154.
56. See Edwards and Stevens, *Lawas and Kanowit*, pp. 51–2.
57 Cramb, 'Agricultural Development', p. 18. It has been suggested that Mitsui Bussan also had monopoly rights in other administrative units but the lack of information renders it difficult to verify this contention. See ibid.
58. Edwards and Stevens, *Lawas and Kanowit*, p. 52.
59. '"Summary Draft of a Policy for the South", Navy National Policy Research Committee, April 1939', Joyce C. Lebra, *Japan's Greater East Asia Co-Prosperity Sphere in World War II: Selected Readings and Documents* (Kuala Lumpur: Oxford University Press, 1975) p. 65.
60. See Sutlive, *Tun Jugah*, pp. 105–6, 167.
61. Edwards and Stevens, *Lawas and Kanowit*, p. 51.
62. Harry Buxton, interview, Aurora Coffee Shop, Kuching, 12 July 1988, cited in Sutlive, *Tun Jugah*, p. 106.
63· Edwards and Stevens, *Lawas and Kanowit*, p. 53.
64. See Lockard, 'Kuching', II, p. 459.
65. Datuk Abang Zainuddin Adi, interview, Kampong Nangka, Sibu, 23 June 1988, cited in Sutlive, *Tun Jugah*, p. 105.
66. '"Summary Draft of a Policy for the South"' in Lebra, *Documents*, p. 65.
67. For mass killings of Chinese in Malaya and Singapore, see Cheah, 'Japanese Occupation', pp. 95–7.
68. K. G. Tregonning, *A History of Modern Sabah (North Borneo 1881–1963)*, 2nd edn (Singapore: University of Malaya Press, 1965) p. 219. For this Chinese-led anti-Japanese insurrection, see 'Information Regarding Position in Nth. Borneo Obtained from Capt. Hamner, 14 April [19]44' (WO 208/1053, PRO); 'Lieut. Kwok and Jesselton Area (from Capt. Hamner's Report)' (WO 208/1053, PRO); 'Guerilla Operations in British North Borneo', Report of Lim King Fatt, Chairman of

the Administrative Board, Overseas Chinese Patriot Guerilla Band and Intelligence Officer of Guerilla Band, to Commanding Officer 125th Infantry Regiment, 10th Military District, 2 November 1943' (WO 208/1053, PRO); and '"How I Happened to Come to Tawi Tawi" by Lim King Fatt, Chairman of the Administrative Board, Overseas Chinese Patriot Guerilla Band and Intelligence Officer of Guerilla Band, to Commanding Officer 125th Infantry Regiment, 10th Military District, 2 November 1943' (WO 208/1053, PRO). See also J. Maxwell-Hall, *Kinabalu Guerillas: An Account of the Double Tenth 1943*, 2nd edn (Kuching: Sarawak Press, 1965).

69. Lockard, 'Kuching', II, p. 457.

70. See Chong Ah Onn, '1943–46, Fifth Division, Sarawak – Part II', *SG*, 31 December 1952, p. 283; and Peter H. H. Howes, *In a Fair Ground or Cibus Cassowarii* (London: Excalibur Press, 1994) p. 168.

71. For details of such forced labour, see for instance, Papers of L. E. Morris (91/18/1, IWM).

72. See for instance, Chin, *Sarawak Chinese*, p. 99. These wartime marriages were one of the contributing factors to a high birth rate during this period which gave Kuching a 10 per cent increase in population. See J. L. Noakes, *Sarawak and Brunei: A Report on the 1947 Population Census* (Kuching: Government Printing Office, 1950), pp. 82–3; *Annual Report on Sarawak for the Year 1947* (Kuching: Government Printing Office, 1948), p. 21; and Craig Alan Lockard, *From Kampung to City: A Social History of Kuching, Malaysia, 1820–1970* (Ohio University Monographs in International Studies, Southeast Asia Series, No. 75, Athens, Ohio: Ohio University Press, 1987) pp. 155–6.

73. A post-war study of the predominantly Malay area of south-west Sarawak (Santubong) showed Chinese migration and settlement during the Japanese period. These Chinese new-comers, mostly from Kuching, lived off the land by growing food crops like *padi* and *ubi kayu* (cassava-manioc), making salt from the sea and sugar from *nipah* palm, and fishing. Some sanctuaries or 'hide-outs' were established in the delta area, the 'heart of nowhere', to avoid the Japanese. See Tom Harrisson, *The Malays of South-West Sarawak Before Malaysia: A Socio-Ecological Survey* (London: Macmillan, 1970) pp. 46–7, 53–4, 301, 303–34, 397, 462, 585, 594–5. For Chinese migration to the inland Land Dayak areas of the Sadong, see 'Monthly Report on Serian and Simunjan District by Capt. D.F.A.F.D. Morgan, Period from 15th February 1946 to 15th March 1946' (WO 203/5983, PRO).

74. See Reece, *The Name of Brooke*, pp. 144–5; Edwards and Stevens, *Lawas abd Kanowit*, p. 53; and James Wong Kim Min (ed.), *'No Joke, James': The World according to William Wong Tsap En* (Singapore: Summer Times Publishing, 1985) pp. 371–3.
75. Peter H. H. Howes, 'The Lintang Camp: Reminiscences of an internee during the Japanese Occupation, 1942–1945', *JMHSSB*, 2 (March 1976) p. 33.
76 For accounts of the experiences of internees, see J. B. Archer, 'Lintang Camp, Kuching, Sarawak. Official Documents and Papers Collected from the Records of the Civilian Internment Camp (No. 1 Camp) at Lintang, Kuching, Sarawak, during the years 1942–1943–1944–1945, Kuching', [1946?] (SMA); K. H. Digby, *Lawyer in the Wilderness* (Cornell University Southeast Asia Program Data Paper No. 114, Ithaca, New York: Cornell University Press, October 1980) pp. 45–70; Howes, *In a Fair Ground* pp. 123–75; Agnes Keith, *Three Came Home* (London: Michael Joseph, 1948); 'Guests of the Japanese', *SG*, 10 August 1950, pp. 204–12; and Ooi Keat Gin, *Japanese Empire in the Tropics: Selected Documents and Reports of the Japanese Period in Sarawak, Northwest Borneo, 1941–1945* (Ohio University Monographs in International Studies, South-East Asian Series, No. 101, Athens, Ohio: Ohio University Press, 1998) II.

Archer and Digby were Brooke officers; Howes served as an Anglican minister among the Land Dayaks of Quop during the pre-war and immediate post-war period; and Mrs Keith was an American married to a forestry official in British North Borneo (Sabah). The account published in the *Sarawak Gazette* is a slightly revised version of a document appended to J. L. Noakes, 'Report Upon Defence Measures Adopted in Sarawak from June 1941 to the Occupation in December 1941 by Imperial Japanese Forces: also, an account of the movement of British and Sarawak Military Forces during the Japanese invasion of Sarawak', 15 February 1946, MSS Pac. s. 62, RHL; from its contents, the authors presumably were Arthur G. Taylor and J. L. Noakes, both Brooke officers. Ooi is a professional historian.

5 The Impact of Japanese Policies on Sarawak's Inhabitants

The British colonial administrators believed that the Malays and the Dayaks [Ibans] had shown markedly different attitudes toward the Japanese invaders. They instinctively felt that whereas the Malays 'treated the Japanese with respect', the Dayaks had 'fiercely resented their presence and did their best to make things difficult for them'. Moreover, when re-occupation began, 'The Dayaks rose in their thousands and took a heavy toll of the Japanese.'[1]

Each ethnic community in Sarawak reacted differently towards the Japanese thanks in part to the different approaches the Japanese adopted towards them. A reciprocal cordiality existed between the Malays and the Japanese whereas covert suspicion and mistrust to a large extent underlaid Chinese-Japanese relations. In other communities, wartime conditions dictated their relationship. However, by the beginning of 1944, the Japanese presence was widely resented by most of Sarawak's inhabitants.

The impact of Japanese wartime policies on the different ethnic groups will be examined, and native-Japanese relations evaluated to determine the extent and influence of these policies and also an analysis of wartime Chinese-Japanese relations in the light of the policies directed towards the Chinese community will be undertaken. For the European community, which spent the war years at Batu Lintang, the focus will be on the impact and consequences of internment/imprisonment as internees and POWs.

ON THE INDIGENOUS PEOPLES

The Malays accepted the Japanese calmly and without expression of resentment. The Malay elite, the *datu* class, either worked willingly (even, in the case of some individuals, enthusiastically) or withdrew from active cooperation as in the case of *Datu Patinggi* Abang Haji Abdillah on the grounds of advanced age. Although some of the educated Iban elite grasped the opportunity offered by the Japanese to occupy positions of authority, the community as a whole resented the Japanese intruders. The Melanaus and the Land Dayaks neither overtly resisted nor outwardly cooperated with the Japanese. The natives of the interior, however, such as the Kayans, Kenyahs, Kelabits, Lun Bawang and Muruts, were hostile to the invaders and readily lent their assistance to the Allies at the very first opportunity.

Despite the prevalence of hardships consequent upon wartime conditions conspicuously prevalent in urban areas, the relations between the Japanese military authorities and the indigenous population were 'uniformly good' up to the latter half of 1944.[2] Towards the closing months of 1944, when 'food shortages, bombing[s], news of the tide turning against JAPAN, and agitation on the part of Allied agents, began to be felt and the population gradually became more and more anti-JAPANESE', resentment grew amongst the people as living conditions worsened with acute shortages in food, clothing and other daily necessities, these were particularly acute among town dwellers.[3] Nevertheless, the anti-Japanese feelings harboured by the majority of Ibans and other indigenes was reserved for the injustices and abuses perpetrated in the implementation of compulsory labour and forced deliveries of rice and other food crops, and the confiscation of firearms.

The Malay community as a whole, town inhabitants as well as the rural peasantry, experienced less hardship than other indigenous groups. As one study indicates, 'The Malays did not prosper during the [Japanese] Occupation but neither did they find it as difficult to survive.'[4] It is argued that 'the Malay standard of living was already, for the great majority, at little better than subsistence level', largely relying on fishing and agriculture, and 'therefore [the Malays] were better prepared than the Chinese to survive during a period of economic hardship'.[5] Furthermore, most Malay police personnel and civil servants remained at their posts under the Japanese military government with the result that their families did not suffer undue privation, both socially and economically.

There were sporadic attempts by the Japanese to gain the 'sympathies of the Mohammedan peoples'[6] which was in line with the general policy towards Islamic peoples in the Southern region, but apparently the majority of Malays and Muslim Melanaus did not subscribe to Japanese propaganda and did not publicly exhibit pro-Japanese sentiments. The Japanese were reported to have distributed rice free of charge to Malay families in Sibu;[7] whether it was done on humanitarian grounds or for propaganda ends, the reasons were unclear. Besides the few individuals who enthusiastically promoted the Japanese cause and worked hand in glove with the new regime, most Malays and other Muslims were oblivious to Japanese rhetoric and propaganda. The general attitude of the community was foccused on surviving the war.

However, when Japanese brutality increased, becoming more evident towards the latter half of the occupation, and the number of incidents of assault on Malay women began to rise,[8] the Malays became more resentful of the Japanese. Nevertheless, no active Malay anti-Japanese opposition, overt or underground, existed.

The Ibans, on the other hand, expressed their resentment of the Japanese in open armed clashes, particularly from the latter half of 1944. Iban alienation was a direct result of Japanese policies: namely, orders confiscating their hunting rifles, forcing them to sell their surplus *padi*, the forced recruitment of adult males into labour gangs for work on military installations, and harsh treatment for petty crimes.

In the aftermath of the Chinese revolt at Jesselton of October 1943, an order was issued by the *Gunseibu* that all firearms should be surrendered. The Ibans were outraged at such a ruling. Non-compliance, however, was met with stern reprisals by the Japanese. A potential Iban anti-Japanese uprising was averted in the Simanggang district by the action of a Japanese police officer, S. Suzuki, who, with the assistance of Eliab Bay, managed to prevent confiscation thereby preventing a major conflict.[9] The Ibans had an opportunity to attack the Japanese when they collaborated in operations with the Australian Services Reconnaissance Department (SRD), the Allied advance parties, when they launched the re-occupation campaign from mid-1945.[10]

The Japanese insistence that surplus rice and other food crops be sold to appointed agents made life burdensome for most natives. Indigenous people in the Lawas district suffered under this ruling when rice supplies had to be brought from the interior:

> Local people would walk to Long Semado ... [to] buy rice from the village, and then carry it back to Lawas [town]. The Japanese permitted each carrier to keep one-half of his load, the other half being given to the government agent, Soon Teck Kongsi, for distribution or export.[11]

In exchange for the surplus rice and other food crops, native farmers received Japanese 'banana' currency, which for the most part was worthless as there were no goods in the bazaar to buy.[12] Nevertheless, in some cases, as in the Saribas, Ibans were offered cloth and clothing for their rice.[13] Some of the more remote longhouses in upriver districts escaped this order. Refusal to abide by this system of forced deliveries meant severe retribution including imprisonment or even death.[14]

Native communities which were unfortunate enough to be singled out as suppliers of coolie labour suffered at the hands of the Japanese who were harsh on workers. In the case of the construction of the Bintulu airfield, the Ibans from the surrounding areas were 'drafted to dig and transport gravel, mix concrete, and perform other heavy tasks'.[15] Apart from the heavy work and ill-treatment, the absence of adult males from the longhouse for long stretches, from two weeks to a

month, 'had adverse consequences for agricultural production ... particularly if the workers were conscripted at a
critical stage of the farming cycle'.[16]

The effects and influences of Japanese-sponsored organizations such as the *kyodotai* and the *jikeidan* were minimal and
inconsequential. These organizations, primarily aimed at promoting and nurturing support and loyalty of the indigenous
peoples to the Japanese regime, had little to show for their
efforts. Both the *kyodotai* and the *jikeidan* were failures.

The ambitious two-year training programme of the *kyodotai*
was not completed. In practice,

> after basic training all trainees were entirely [us]ed to assist
> various JAPANESE undertakings such as the building of
> factories and camps, the [d]riv[ing] and maintaining of
> JAPANESE vehicles and in cultivating land to produce crops
> designed to fill the belly of the JAPANESE soldiery.[17]

The objectives of the *kyodotai* were not attained; it was
disbanded in August 1945. According to Captain Ryuji Ikeno,
the commander of the Miri Company, its failure was attrib-
uted to the following reasons.

a) The dislike of the natives for the JAPANESE.
b) Unpleasant character of some of the JAPANESE soldiers
   in charge of training.
c) On both sides, the language difficulty was an ever-
   present obstacle.
d) The period of training was too short.
e) The unfavourable situation of JAPANESE in the war at
   the end of 1944 caused the native soldiers to lose interest in the course and they ran away whenever they
   could.
f) Gradually, owing to air raids causing dislocation of
   communication and lack of food, duties became more
   and more arduous; education was neglected and
   discipline languished.[18]

Moreover the free-spirited nature of the natives, especially
that of the Ibans, could not easily adjust to the harsh and

strict discipline demanded by the Japanese. Consequently, not surprisingly, many disillusioned natives deserted their *kyodotai* units; some not only deserted their posts but defected to the SRD to help it in its campaign against the Japanese.[19]

Equally disappointing was the *jikeidan* organization. The longhouses in the interior districts, instead of functioning as an informal espionage network feeding information to Japanese intelligence, instead provided valuable assistance and logistical support to SRD operations. Despite the threat of severe punishment, longhouses in the Limbang offered shelter and protection for downed American airmen in late 1944. The natives, consequently, paid dearly for their defiance.[20]

The efforts to popularize the virtues of the 'Greater East Asia Co-Prosperity Sphere' and other Japanese propaganda designed to win over the indigenous peoples to the Japanese cause met with little success. As pointed out, the attempts at gaining the support of the Muslim inhabitants were generally abortive. Despite the dissemination of propaganda materials in the vernacular, namely in Malay (and to a lesser extent in Iban), their influence and effects were inconsequential. Among the plausible reasons for Japanese failure to gain the support of the indigenous population were the general harshness of the military government and the implementation of unpopular policies that alienated most of the native communities. The two major probable causes of the ineffectiveness of Japanese propaganda, however, are the high illiteracy rate among indigenous peoples and their general disinterest in politics.[21]

Instruction in *Nippon-go*, as a carrier of Japanese propaganda, also did not meet with much success among native peoples. By virtue of the fact that classes were mostly based in the towns, 'a fairly high percentage of the urban population will have acquired at least a rudimentary knowledge of Japanese', but the majority of native inhabitants in the rural areas remained untouched by this development.[22] Even using Malay and Iban as the medium of propaganda was ineffective;

printed leaflets and pamphlets in Malay or in Iban extolling the virtues of Japanese rule and hatred for the Allies which were distributed proved a vain exercise in a country where the illiteracy rate was high.

The failure of Japanese propaganda among the indigenous population is clearly exemplified by the loyalty they professed for the former Brooke regime. The native peoples, especially those in the hilly and remote interior, expressed their fidelity by assisting and participating in SRD operations.

Notwithstanding the non-fulfilment of many of Japanese intentions towards indigenous peoples, the period of occupation did produce some beneficial effects for natives, particularly for the Ibans. The Brookes had done little to emplace Ibans and other non-Malay natives as civil administrators and in the police force. The Japanese, on the other hand, promoted the few Ibans who joined the police force just before the war to positions of 'considerable responsibility'.

The Japanese implementation of indirect rule in the Second Division produced the most celebrated example of an Iban holding a high administrative position in the military government. Eliab Bay, the Iban who was appointed 'Liaison Officer' for the Second Division based in Simanggang, wielded considerable administrative power and influence. Bay was, in practice, occupying the position of a 'Resident', an exclusively European appointment during Brooke times; he was able to appoint *guncho*, a power which he utilized to elevate other Ibans in the administrative hierarchy. 'An outcome of all this', as one scholar commented, 'was that the educated Ibans employed by the Japanese realized that they were fully capable of taking a responsible part in the administration of the country'.[23]

The Japanese policy of retaining native police personnel and civil administrators afforded these individuals an opportunity to prove their capabilities in the absence of European tutelage. In the outstations particularly, the conspicuous lack of Japanese personnel meant that there were few, if any, Japanese officers on the spot, thereby allowing Malay and Iban civil and police officials to administer whole districts

entirely on their own. Although they were subjected to
nominal Japanese supervision and alerted to occasional military patrols, these native officers experienced a new sense of
independence not imagined possible in Brooke days. Such
experiences undoubtedly contributed to their confidence as
administrators. The wartime experiences of these selected
Ibans had a significant effect on their self-confidence as
administrators; but more important, was the development of
their political consciousness.[24]

Another positive effect of the Japanese period on
the indigenous communities was the achievement of self-
sufficiency in food crop production, namely rice. Native
farmers not only produced enough rice for their own needs
but also had surpluses for sale to *Gunseibu* appointed agents.

Since the 1870s there had been shortages in domestic
output of rice, the staple food of the population, and the
dependence on imported rice continued until 1941 despite
all the efforts expanded by the Brooke administration to
address this shortcoming. Chinese peasant farmers from
South China were invited to establish farming settlements in
the Lower Rejang at the turn of the century with the aim that
these immigrants would boost local rice production. Prior to
the commercial cultivation of rubber, rice shortages affected
the urban population and mining centres where the bulk of the
Chinese population relied primarily on imported rice for
their sustenance. Native communities living in the rural districts were subsistence rice farmers (wet-rice or hill/dry rice)
and only resorted to imported rice in times of poor harvests
or crop failures. However, the introduction of rubber cultivation, a more lucrative and less labour-intensive activity,
displaced rice cultivation even among native farmers and
Chinese immigrants in the Lower Rejang. Boom rubber
prices encouraged expansion of rubber clearings at the
expanse of rice fields. In spite of the rice crisis of 1919–21,
followed by the slump in rubber prices of the early 1920s, and
the Depression (1929–31), native and Chinese alike continued to have faith in rubber. Brooke attempts at achieving
self-sufficiency in rice remained unfulfilled.[25]

The Japanese policy of stressing self-sufficiency in food supplies and the use of coercion in its implementation spurred indigenous farmers into producing rice and other food crop surpluses. From mid-1944 the food supply situation became particularly acute when Japanese shipping was increasingly disrupted by Allied successes in the Pacific. Greater stress was then placed on attaining food self-sufficiency. In addition to Japanese pressure, other factors also contributed to the achievement of self-sufficiency in rice and other food supplies. With practically no demand for rubber, Malay and Iban farmers moved into rice growing on a larger scale. Other food crops such as tapioca, sago, vegetables and fruits also received attention with increased output. Nature too played its part during the occupation period when farmers were blessed with good harvests. The Ibans considered these years as 'cool' or 'stable' (*taun celap*) during which good crops (*bulih padi*) were obtained.[26] Notwithstanding the coercive nature of forced deliveries of surpluses, native rice farmers reported a 'minor boom'.[27]

The Japanese military administration did achieve its goal of food self-sufficiency by making Sarawak 'more or less self-sufficient in food for the first time in over 70 years'.[28] The Japanese succeeded where the Brookes had failed.

ON THE CHINESE COMMUNITY

Considering the dominant position of the Chinese in trade and commerce prior to the occupation, wartime conditions adversely affected their livelihood. In order to achieve greater control over food supplies and other commodities, the Japanese commandeered some trading shops, effected mergers, and appointed some merchant houses to carry out work as contract companies. Typical of such a situation is this example from Lawas of the aforementioned Soon Teck Kongsi:

Then after a few months into 1942, the Japanese decided that one shop should handle all the trade for the District.

The agent selected was Soon Teck Kongsi, a combination of two of the most prominent shops in Lawas at that time, Guan Soon and Hoon Teck. The new shop would not accept purchase orders; it only distributed Japanese goods and collected produce brought in by farmers in the District.[29]

Meanwhile in Sundar and Trusan, a Taiwanese was appointed as agent for collecting foodstuffs in these two districts for the Japanese.[30]

The Japanese emphasis on self-sufficiency in food supplies and the demand for food crops had a positive effect on some Chinese farmers who were able to demand high prices for their produce. In league with the Chinese businessmen in the towns who willingly cooperated with the Japanese, these farmers performed well in disposing of their agricultural produce (vegetables, poultry, rice), achieving prosperity at the expense of their fellow countrymen.[31] On balance, Chinese rural farming communities fared better than their urban counterparts. In the remote district of Limbang, for instance, the Chinese suffered little from food shortages and were generally well provided for from their own farms even after the forced deliveries to the Japanese military. Chinese in neighbouring Lawas were also adequately supplied by their own farm.[32]

Apart from the highly resented prosperity of the several Chinese traders, some farmers, and those involved in smuggling and the black market, the majority suffered setbacks during the occupation. Trade came almost to a standstill from mid-1944 when the Japanese take-over of shops, and the crippling demands for cash donations (a staggering $2 million), reversed the fortunes of many Chinese trading concerns. Many middle-class Chinese who relied on their savings, on the sale of their jewellery and other valuables, and who had no recourse to other sources of income, were in dire straits when the war ended.

The Chinese as a whole were politically indifferent prior to the Japanese invasion. But witnessing the collapse of the Raj, the indelible scene of the procession of European Brooke officers being marched into internment camps, and the ignominious flight of British forces across the border into Dutch south-west Borneo, fostered the heightening of nationalistic feelings within the Chinese community. What is more, observing Malay and Iban police personnel and Native Officers (mostly Malays) remaining at their posts while some were even promoted (a clear indication of collaborating with the occupying forces) combined with the disillusionment with their own community leaders who apparently were cooperating with the enemy, spread indignation and disgust among the Chinese. However, the resentment by the Chinese which provoked their political awakening did not manifest itself in overt anti-Japanese activities during the occupation, but was undoubtedly brewing throughout this period, only becoming apparent in the immediate post-war years (and particularly during the tumultuous decade of the 1950s).

ON THE EUROPEAN COMMUNITY

Apart from the few individuals who succeeded in escaping to Australia, practically the entire European community in Sarawak spent the war years behind the barbed wire fence that enclosed Batu Lintang Camp. Although there were undoubtedly great hardships in terms of physical survival as a result of the shortages in all aspects of living necessities from food to clothing to medicine for the sick, the civilian internees fared better than their POW counterparts, and the women were in better condition than the men. A female internee explained this discrepancy as follows: 'We women draw the same rations as the soldiers, which though insufficient, serves us better than the male prisoners, who do manual labour, and in any case, need more than the female sex.'[33] Furthermore,

> The [British] soldiers are treated very badly by the Nips [Japanese], and are underfed and overworked. Originally

they had been sent to Malaya after only six months training in England, and many were far from sturdy, or in the A1. [medical] category. Before becoming acclimatised to tropical conditions they were taken prisoner, – many without having fired a shot.

Soon many of these men exchanged their clothing and other items for food and tobacco, but many lost heart and just died ... the majority are simply human skeletons with listless eyes, crawling feebly about their tasks. There are no medical dressings, and many have filthy ulcers, and large sores exposed on their hips.

The men are covered with mosquito bites which have turned septic, and also have scabies. The fatless diet is the main cause of many of their skin conditions.[34]

Despite such trying conditions both arrogance and cockiness verging on stupidity were exhibited by some Europeans during the years of internment. Several civilian internees insisting that 'the Japanese should supply' all food requirements, refused to grow food on land allocated for this purpose, with resultant suffering for all concerned. The detractors argued that 'the Japanese would take it all, and though they were proved wrong in the end, nevertheless their influence did much to retard gardening and reduce our much needed green food supply'.[35] Others who were opposed even created obstructions for 'those who were public spirited enough to work to produce food for the community'.[36]

Then there was an exhibition of naivete on the part of the POWs and other internees who were assigned work to repair and rebuilt the landing grounds. Initially a note of protest was made to the Japanese regarding such work on military installations which they felt transgressed the Hague Convention of 1907 for treatment of POWs (although they were uncertain whether Japan was a signatory):

Kassia [Japanese Officer] arrived about nine a.m. and as soon as he heard of our complaint he jumped on to a trolley and entangled his sword in his legs – fell off – got on again and then, through a bad interpreter, said 'Siapa yang tida mahu kerja, pergi sa blah sini [Whoever refuse to work, move across to this place],' indicating a vacant space to one side. Five men stepped across, but the rest of our Company, including those so firmly resolved the night before not to work for the Japanese, stayed where they were. Mr. Verheul, the Dutch representative, tried to explain that we were not objecting to work, but to this particular type of work, and was briskly slapped for his pains. Kassia then informed us that whoever refused to work would be shot, and Mr. Verheul, seeing the hopelessness of any concerted refusal, ordered the lonely four to return to the other side. In the evening we were all paraded and addressed by Kassia. He informed us that we would work wherever we were ordered and death by shooting would be the penalty for refusing. Martyrdom did not appeal to us.[37]

Although beatings and other physical abuse were reported, none of the recipients was severely incapacitated permanently as a result. Even the victim of *Kempeitai* treatment did not suffer any permanent physical damage; although the psychological scars undoubtedly remained for a long time.[38]

As far as was reported there was only one single case of rape involving a European female; Miss D. Were, a fourteen-year-old-girl, was sexually assaulted by five Japanese soldiers during the time she and her family were arrested. She was treated at the hospital after the incident. Although it is difficult to confirm, apparently one of the rapists was later imprisoned and 'badly thrashed at different times by the Japanese police'.[39] Surprisingly there were no reports, or even allusions, of incidents of molestation or rape by the Japanese camp wardens and soldiers on European female internees at Batu Lintang Camp.[40] Such fortunate circumstances were due to the strict discipline kept by the Japanese commandant, Lieutenant Colonel Suga, over his men. Apparently Suga had a 'soft spot' for women and children; he allowed the children to ride in his staff car within the compounds of the camp![41]

Life under internment revealed many facets of human nature. Despite the struggle to stay alive, there were still other matters which were deemed far more important than survival. Vanity was not dead. A clear example can be seen when 'the wives would put on any make-up they might still possess, and don any garment which had been preserved' for the occasions of meeting their husbands.[42] One woman internee muses on how it will be 'interesting to see oneself in a full sized mirror', and worriedly reflects that, 'The others seem to have lost their female curves, and all of us go *in* where we should go *out*'![43] 'I wonder', she adds, 'whether fashions have changed very much during the years we have been here'.[44]

If vanity was not dead, enterprise and charity were very much alive. Starting from a few chicks, one male internee (in partnership with three others) boasted that 'in August 1945, we had 31 hens in our possession. Very often we used to give eggs to our more chronic sick in our company and this was well appreciated.'[45]

Necessity is indeed the mother of invention. There was no lack of ingenuity and creativity. Notwithstanding the severe penalty, acts of defiance (ranging from keeping a diary/journal to assembling a radio from scratch and operating it under the noses of the Japanese with the help of a camp-constructed generator) exhibited the ingenuity of human nature under extreme circumstances.[46] The birth of 'The Old Lady' (also known as 'Mrs Harris'), the made-in-camp radio, and her companion, 'Ginnie', the made-in-camp generator, and their operation under the noses of the Japanese testified to the ingenuity and resourcefulness of humankind under extremely critical situations where discovery meant manda-tory death. Morale was boosted, at best kept alive, when news reported by the 'Old Lady' was disseminated. The ingenuity in the face of extreme adversity in creating the 'Old Lady', and her companion 'Ginnie', are testimonies to humankind's determination for survival. No doubt there were many close shaves and heart-stopping moments for those involved, but their efforts, and the rather inventive dissemination of news through the Chaplain (Padre) gave hope to many to continue their fight for survival. Hope is a tonic for living. The culmination of their triumph was undoubtedly the presentation before Suga's eyes of the 'Old Lady' and 'Ginnie'![47]

For the sake of survival individuals are willing to perform many things: from selling a wedding ring to stealing from a dead comrade. Owing to hunger, a male internee decided to sell his gold wedding ring; a transaction was effected in the black market through an intermediary. The money obtained from this sale, amounting to $45, was use to buy 'some coconut oil, one or two eggs and a few bananas'.[48] Likewise, hunger pangs drove two internees to risk their lives to rob a dead colleague in his grave. An observer recorded this episode of the struggle for survival:

> The grave they seek is not very deep and the earth covering the body is lightly packed. Burial parties lack the necessary strength to dig deep graves and the earth which covers the body is always hurriedly returned.
>
> Quickly the two set about the task of removing sufficient earth to enable them to reach the body. But they have frequent stops to rest and breathe, for their breathing is loud and laboured and can easily be heard on this still and eerie night.
>
> 'I've got him, quick give a hand', I overhear.
>
> A macabre struggle follows before an arm of the body is finally extracted and the gold ring quickly slipped from its finger.
>
> Hurriedly the men return the partially exhumed body and replace the scattered earth until the grave again looks undisturbed.
>
> The following morning at the working party on Kuching aerodrome they make their sale and receive in return a supply of coconut oil and a few eggs.
>
> This will guarantee them a few more days survival.[49]

When it comes to life or death situations, the instinctive pursuit of survival overrides whatever moral qualms therein. It is difficult, or perhaps even unfair, to apply moral judgements over such acts under such trying circumstances.

The total population of Batu Lintang Camp was about 3000 POWs, consisting of British, Australian, Dutch and Indian Army men. By the time of liberation in September 1945, 750 were alive, out of which only 50 were fit for work.[50] One source recorded '1,387' as 'Alive in Kuching area', presumably referring to Batu Lintang.[51] The civilian survivors numbered 1145, of which 242 were women and children.

CONCLUSION

The Japanese practised the principle of 'divide and rule' as well as the tenets of indirect rule over Sarawak. Communal leaders were utilized as go-betweens by the *Gunseibu* to garner the support and cooperation of the various ethnic groups. Indirect rule was practised in the Iban-dominated Second Division by promoting a handful of educated Ibans to positions of responsibility. By using this strategy the *Gunseibu* managed to optimize administrative control using non-Japanese personnel and with minimum Japanese resources. Such a practice proved effective throughout the wartime period.

Different communities reacted differently to Japanese policies. The Japanese failed to win over the indigenous peoples to their cause, instead, in some cases, like the confiscation of firearms, the natives felt driven to oppose them. But from another perspective, the coercive action of the Japanese succeeded in forcing the natives to produce sufficient rice and other food crops to meet the demands of the Japanese military and the requirements of the local population, and yet allowed some surplus. Such an achievement in rice self-sufficiency has yet to be equalled by any pre-war or post-war government. The Japanese to a large extent succeeded in cowing the Chinese community and secured the cooperation of the communal leadership and the collaboration of certain ambitious sectors of the community. Although extremely deprived of food and medicine for the sick, and subjected to harsh working conditions and repeated beatings, the majority of European internees and POWs did not lose hope in the fight for survival. Thanks to a daring few, outside news via the made-in-camp radio operated by a made-in-camp generator kept up morale and gave hope to those on the verge of giving up the struggle to live.

Comparatively, the brief Japanese period in Sarawak had less impact on the various ethnic groups than post-war developments within the country and events from without. Nationalistic consciousness among the Malays manifested itself during the cession issue. Heightened Chinese nationalism became apparent towards the late 1940s which was dictated more from developments in the mainland and influenced to a lesser extent by local events. Sarawak Chinese nationalism and patriotism towards the motherland which emerged hand in hand with the increasing influence of Leftist elements within the Chinese community will be discussed in the next chapter.

Notes

1. Michael B. Leigh, *The Rising Moon: Political Change in Sarawak* (Sydney: Sydney University Press, 1974) p. 32. Part of quote is from C. W. Dawson, Chief Secretary of Sarawak, Private Papers, 25 November 1947 (typescript).
2. 'Intelligence Bulletin No.237, Item 2183: Interrogation of Lieutenant-General Masao BABA, General Officer Commanding 37th Army' (WO 203/6317, PRO) p. 19.
3. Ibid.
4. C. A. Lockard, 'The Southeast Asian Town in Historical Perspective: A Social History of Kuching, Malaysia, 1820–1970' (PhD thesis, University of Wisconsin, 1973) II, p. 460.
5. Ibid., pp. 460–1.
6. 'British Territories in North Borneo', extract from Allied Land Forces South-East Asia (A.L.F.S.E.A.), Wartime Intelligence Report (W.I.R.), No. 52, 28 September 1945 (WO 208/105, PRO) p. 22.
7. See Liew Yung Tzu, *Sarawak Under the Japanese* (Sibu: Hua Ping Press, 1956) [text in Chinese] p. 30, cited by Lockard, 'Kuching', II, p. 461.
8. See Craig Alan Lockard, *From Kampung to City: A Social History of Kuching, Malaysia, 1820–1970* (Ohio University

Monographs in International Studies, Southeast Asia Series, No. 75, Athens, Ohio: Ohio University Press, 1987) p. 153.

9. For his part, Suzuki 'was under threat of repatriation and court-martial for defying orders': R. H. W. Reece, *The Name of Brooke: The End of White Rajah Rule in Sarawak* (Kuala Lumpur: Oxford University Press, 1982) p. 149.

10. In early 1945, SRD units were parachuted behind enemy lines in central and north-east Borneo to organize resistance in preparation for Allied landings. They recruited Kayans, Kenyahs, Kelabits and Muruts for their offensive operations against the Japanese. When these operations reached the Rejang, Ibans joined in the fight. The SRD also received assistance, including recruits, from the Chinese. For SRD operations, see Tom Harrisson, *World Within: A Borneo Story* (London: The Cresset Press, 1959); and Bob Long, *Operation Semut 1:'Z' Special Unit's Secret War; Soldiering with the Head-Hunters of Borneo* (Maryborough, Victoria: Australian Print Group, 1989).

11. Leonard Edwards and Peter W. Stevens, *Short Histories of the Lawas and Kanowit Districts* (Kuching: Borneo Literature Bureau, 1971) p. 55.

12. Ibid., p. 56.

13. See R. A Cramb, 'The Impact of the Japanese Occupation on Agricultural Development in Sarawak', 1994/1995 MS (Personal Copy) p. 20.

14. Violators of this ruling about delivering rice surplus to the government agent in the Lawas district were 'sent to the central prison in Brunei and a few of those never returned': Edwards and Stevens, *Lawas and Kanowit*, p. 56.

15. Vinson H. Sutlive, Jr. *Tun Jugah of Sarawak: Colonialism and Iban Response* (Kuala Lumpur: Penerbit Fajar Bakti for Sarawak Literary Society, 1992) p. 107.

16. Cramb, 'Agricultural Development', p. 9.

17. 'Intelligence Bulletin No. 237, Item 2182: Interrogation of Lieutenants Yoshihiko WAKAMATSU and Kenzo MORIKAWA, and Captains Ryuji IKENO, Minoru TASUMA and Yoshio WATANABE, all officers attached to the North Borneo Volunteer Corps (KYODOTAI); Subject: North Borneo Volunteer Corps; c. mid-1946' (WO 203/6317, PRO) p. 12.

18. Ibid., p. 13.

19. See Chong Ah Onn, '1943–46, Fifth Division, Sarawak – Pt.II', *SG*, 31 December 1952, p. 285.

20. In the closing months of 1944, a US plane crashed in Telak in the Limbang district. For this episode which ended tragically for some of the rescuers and the rescued, see 'Heroism in the Limbang', *SG*, 2 June 1947, pp. 100–1.

21. See 'British Territories in North Borneo', p. 24.

    Thanks to Brooke *laissez-faire* educational policy, the percentage of the non-Muslim indigenous population who partook of schooling in Christian mission schools was less than 5 per cent of the total native population. The Malays in the urban areas had a higher literacy rate than their rural cousins, but still the percentage of literates was no more than 15 per cent. See Ooi Keat Gin, 'Mission Education in Sarawak During the Period of Brooke Rule, 1841–1946', *SMJ*, 42, 63 (December 1991) 324–33; and 'Sarawak Malay Attitudes Towards Education During the Brooke Period, 1841–1946', *JSEAS*, 21, 2 (September 1990) 350–9.

22. 'British Territories in North Borneo', p. 24.
23. See Reece, *Name of Brooke*, p. 147.
24. See Reece, *Name of Brooke*, pp. 147–8; and Leigh, *The Rising Moon*, pp. 32–3.
25. For a detailed study of Brooke rice self-sufficiency policy, see Ooi Keat Gin, 'For Want of Rice: Sarawak's Attempts at Rice Self-Sufficiency During the Period of Brooke Rule, 1841–1941', *JSEAS* 29, 1 (March 1998) 8–23.
26. See *SG*, 2 September 1946, p. 9; and Cramb, 'Agricultural Development', p. 20.
27. Ong, *Department of Agriculture 1941–1945*, cited in Cramb, 'Agricultural Development', p. 19.
28. Cramb, 'Agricultural Development', p. 30.
29. Edwards and Stevens, *Lawas and Kanowit*, p. 52.
30. See Chong, '1943–46, Fifth Division, Sarawak – Part II', p. 285. For the situation in Kuching, see Lockard, 'Kuching', II, p. 458.
31. For instance, see Chong, '1943–46, Fifth Division, Sarawak – Part I', *SG*, 29 November 1952, p. 264; and John M. Chin, *The Sarawak Chinese* (Kuala Lumpur: Oxford University Press, 1981) pp. 99–100.
32. See James Wong Kim Min (ed.), *'No Joke, James': The World according to William Wong Tsap En* (Singapore: Summer Times Publishing, 1985) pp. 375, 379, 386, 409–10, 412; and Edwards and Stevens, *Lawas and Kanowit*, p. 54.
33. Papers of Miss H. E. Bates (MSS 91/35/1 IWM) p. 101.
34. Ibid.
35. J. L. Noakes, 'Personal Report Upon My Experiences While Interned from 24th December 1941 to the 16th September 1945', attached to J. L. Noakes, 'Report Upon Defence Measures Adopted in Sarawak from June 1941 to the Occupation in December 1941 by Imperial Japanese Forces; also, an account of the movement of British and Sarawak Military Forces during the Japanese invasion of Sarawak', 15 February 1946 (MSS Pac. s. 62, RHL) p. 5.

36. Noakes, 'Personal Report', p. 5.
37. Ibid., p. 4.
38. Sapper Lionel E. Morris of the Royal Engineers who was interned as a POW at Batu Lintang Camp had the unfortunate fate of being caught by the *Kempeitai* for keeping a diary. Miraculously he survived *Kempeitai* 'hospitality', and returned physically unscathed from the experience. See the Papers of L. E. Morris (91/18/1, IWM) pp. 172–88.
39. Noakes, 'Report Upon Defence Measures', pp. 66–7.
40. Agnes Newton Keith, one of the female internees of Batu Lintang Camp, described in her autobiographical book *Three Came Home* (London: Michael Joseph, 1948) an attempted rape on her by a Japanese guard (pp. 145–7) which it is difficult to substantiate. Attempts to corroborate Keith's accusation with the memoirs and recollections of other women internees failed to ascertain that such an incident did happen; even a mere rumour alluding to such an occurrence did not emerge.
41. See 'Report No. 2 – Kuching', 6 October 1945, HQ Kuching Forces, 9 Australian Division Australian Imperial Force (AIF) to Director of Naval Intelligence, Navy Office, Melbourne (WO 208/1054, PRO).
42. Papers of Miss H. E. Bates (MSS 91/35/1, IWM) p. 95.
43. Ibid., p. 109.
44. Ibid., p. 112.
45. Papers of E. R. Pepler (88/33/1, IWM) p. 22.
46. See ibid., pp. 10–18; and Papers of G. W. Pringle (IWM) pp. 158–286.
47. For the risks and daring defiance, and the genius in creating a radio and generator from scratch, see Ooi Keat Gin, *Japanese Empire in the Tropics: Selected Documents and Reports of the Japanese Period in Sarawak, Northwest Borneo, 1941–1945*, 2 vols. (Ohio University Monographs in International Studies, South-East Asian Series, No. 101, Athens, Ohio: Ohio University Press, 1998) II, pp. 439–522.
48. Papers of G. W. Pringle (IWM) p. 217.
49. Ibid., pp. 240–1.
50. See Ivor M. Purden, 'Japanese P.O.W. Camps in Borneo', in *Borneo: The Japanese P.O.W. Camps – Mail of the Forces, P.O.W. and Internees*, Neville Watterson (Wellingborough: W. N. Watterson, 1989) p. 22.
51. See Papers of Miss H. E. Bates (MSS 91/35/1, IWM) p. 119.

6 The Japanese Period and its Effects on Post-War Developments

Following two inconclusive naval battles in the Coral Sea and near Midway Island, Japan found itself gradually losing the supremacy of the sea which it had commanded since Pearl Harbor. It was the Allies' turn to inflict damage on Japanese shipping to the Southern Area. The initial Allied strategy was to bypass the Philippines, Borneo and Java, and head straight for Japan by means of 'island hopping'. However, military strategy was overruled by political considerations. The US President, Franklin Roosevelt, decided that it was politically advantageous to American post-war policy to honour General Douglas MacArthur's promise to return to the Philippines. Therefore, in the revised Allied plans, the responsibility for retaking former British North Borneo, Brunei, Sarawak and Dutch Borneo was entrusted to the AIF 9th Division. The re-capture of Borneo was part of MacArthur's strategy to secure bases for the invasion of Java.[1]

The Borneo campaign was launched in early May 1945 with a brigade of the Australian 9th Division landing in Tarakan, Dutch Borneo. Other sections of the 9th Division headed for Brunei Bay and Labuan with landings in early June. The major landing by the bulk of the Australian 7th Division was reserved for Balikpapan in Dutch Borneo which was effected on 1 July. Ample naval and air support provided by the Americans prepared the Australian landings.[2]

Prior to the main AIF landings, personnel from SRD 'Z' Special Unit were dropped behind enemy lines in Central Borneo.[3] Within Sarawak, the *Semut* Operations of the SRD performed remarkably well in terms of the extensive area they covered, the small losses in personnel, and the large number of enemy casualties.[4]

The Australian 9th Division successfully drove the Japanese into the interior. In some cases, the Australians were assisted by the SRD and their local allies, namely the indigenous peoples of the interior such as the Kayans, Kenyahs and Muruts, who were later joined by the Ibans and Chinese.

Abruptly the war started, and abruptly it ended.

The atomic bombing of Hiroshima followed by Nagasaki, and Japan's unconditional surrender thereafter cut short the fighting and brought a sudden end to the Pacific War. Following VP-Day, (Victory in the Pacific) 15 August 1945, several Japanese garrisons continued the struggle; by early November, however, the last of the Japanese units finally surrendered.[5] Notwithstanding the fighting in the interior, the official Japanese surrender in Sarawak took place on 11 September 1945, during a ceremony held on board His Majesty's Australian Ship (HMAS) *Kapunda* at Kuching. The Australians received the surrender of Japanese forces in Borneo.

Plate 6.1   Japanese soldiers on their way to Krokong, on the outskirts of Kuching, at the end of the war (*courtesy the late Sir Thomas Eastick*)

Plate 6.2 Major-General Hiyoe Yamamura, commander of Japanese forces in the Kuching area, arriving on board HMAS *Kapunda* to sign the surrender documents, September 1945 (*courtesy the late Sir Thomas Eastick*)

Meanwhile, the Royal Australian Air Force (RAAF) dropped medical supplies, food and clothing to internment and POW camps throughout its sectors of operation which included Sarawak. Internees of Batu Lintang gratefully and happily partook of these supplies.

Following the surrender, it was decided to send an advance force to Kuching accompanied by personnel from the civil affairs unit consisting mainly of ex-Sarawak officers. The object of this mission was to evacuate the POWs and civilian internees of Batu Lintang Camp. There was a fear that there might be a repeat of the Ranau genocide where the Japanese in former British North Borneo, seeing the tide of war turning against them, decided to turn on their captives of about 2750 Australian and British POWS.[6] But, fortunately for the inmates of Batu Lintang, nothing of such devilish intention was realised.[7]

However, as the prisoners and internees were overwhelmingly European, it was thought 'that the Asia[n] population would take a dim view of the Europeans being taken away and of their being left to the mercy of the Japanese military command'.[8] Under such circumstances, it was commendable to note that the civil affairs company volunteered to stay behind in Kuching without supporting troops. The inmates of Batu Lintang were sent to Labuan where those needing medical attention were treated while others enjoyed recuperation and relaxation. When transport was available these former internees and POWs were sent home.

It was only in September that an Australian task force of the 9th Division, Kuching Force, under the command of Brigadier Thomas C. Eastick, landed in Kuching. The administration was handed over to the Australian forces. In November the British Military Administration (BMA) assumed control. Several experienced officers of the Sarawak Brooke government served in the BMA, and their presence 'gave confidence to the [local] people who were not unnaturally in a state of mind which was ready to be suspicious of anything new'.[9]

Though their tenure was brief, the BMA did a marvellous job, particularly in re-establishing health and other essential services.[10] The people wholeheartedly welcomed the food and other necessities supplied by the BMA. It was no wonder that an old Iban commenting on the issue of cession, declared his preference: 'The Rajah's Government was good, and we feel that the King's Government will be good, but the Government we really would like is the B.M.A.'[11]

Rajah Vyner and Ranee Sylvia returned to Kuching in April 1946. Civil government was resumed under the Rajah and a few of his officers. Several old familiar faces of the pre-war Brooke civil service who had survived happily returned to serve the Raj.

Following a series of discussions between the Rajah's government and the British government dating back to 1943 and 1944 and culminating in the passing of the Cession Bill of 17 May 1946 by Council Negri, Sarawak was ceded to Britain and became a British Crown Colony on 1 July 1946.[12] Sir Charles Noble Arden Clarke became the first colonial governor.

FACING THE QUISLING PROBLEM

[I]t was obvious that many people who could be said to have collaborated with the Japanese, had really done no more than their duty to the public by staying at their posts. It was never intended that everybody should down tools directly the occupation commenced. These people could not possibly have been prosecuted, but it was not easy to draw lines between those who had worked for the Japanese because they had a family to support (the great majority), and those who so worked because they wished to assist the Japanese war effort (a small minority), and, lastly, those who so worked in order to act as a buffer between the governed and their new governors (hardly a handful).[13]

A series of post-war administration – Australian occupying forces, British Borneo Civil Affairs Unit (BBCAU, a unit of the BMA), Brooke government, and Colonial Office – had to face the sensitive issue of collaboration and the awaited punishment of those involved. The collaboration issue had several repercussions, one of which was the disruption of communal relations.

The collaboration issue affected the Malay community more than any other indigenous group. The Malays had offered the least opposition to the Japanese regime and in turn suffered comparatively less than other ethnic communities. Their leaders, too, could be numbered among the 'small minority' who zealously and enthusiastically bent more than the customary forty-five degrees to the image of His Imperial Majesty the Emperor of Japan. But the Malays at the same time were the acknowledged ruling class, and accordingly were incorporated into the pre-war Brooke administrative structure. Therefore the post-1946 British Colonial government was faced with a dilemma on the issue of Malay collaborators.

The re-instated Brooke government, ever indulgent towards the Malays, was sympathetic and understanding to the last towards this 'small minority'. Rajah Vyner, who returned to Kuching in April 1946 admitted that several of the Malay *datu* were 'not too good' during the Japanese period. 'They all ran away to start with', he told Bertram, the Tuan Muda, 'and eventually returned festooned with Jap[anese] medals. But one can't be hard on our Malays – it wasn't really their war.'[14] On the one hand, the 'small minority' of pro-Japanese Malay leaders could not be prosecuted 'since there were no friendlier people with equal authority to put in their places'.[15] However, the British authorities could not, on the other hand, 'afford to prosecute the lesser fry and leave the big fish untouched', for 'Too many rude comparisons would have been drawn for anybody's comfort. The only course [therefore] was to let them all go on swimming safely together.'[16] The post-1946 British Colonial government decided on the latter course, and instructions were issued 'not to institute further proceedings against persons alleged to be guilty of collaboration with the enemy ... where no atrocities or brutality is involved'.[17]

Although prominent Malay 'collaborators' escaped unscathed, their Iban counterparts faced rougher times from the British colonial authorities. Eliab Bay, for instance, was dismissed from government service, while Juing Insol, a policeman who gained rapid promotion under the Japanese, 'could well have become Commissioner for Police had it not been for his reputation as a particularly anti-British collaborator'.[18] Unlike the more politicized Malays, which the cession issue had demonstrated, the British Colonial government could afford to ride roughshod over the handful of Iban collaborators without fear of unwelcome repercussion. From the support and cooperation rendered by the Ibans and other indigenes of the interior to the SRD operatives towards the closing years of the war, the British colonial authorities knew for certain where Iban loyalties lay. Since the majority of Ibans and other native peoples were staunchly anti-Japanese, and more importantly, pro-British, identifying and persecuting known collaborators would not bring forth any untoward negative reaction towards the newly installed colonial administration. These Iban collaborators were themselves unpopular amongst their community for their wartime (mis)behaviour. Any mistreatment, or even incarceration, of these individuals by the colonial authorities would be welcomed by the Iban community themselves and also by the wider public.

THE DECLINE OF TRADITIONAL NATIVE LEADERSHIP

It is uncertain whether the action of the British Colonial government in ending the special privilege accorded Malays and the removal of preference for that group in civil service appointments was a reaction to Malay collaboration during the occupation period, their opposition to Sarawak's cession to the British Crown, or simply a move to break with Brooke tradition and establish a more egalitarian administrative bureaucracy open to all ethnic groups.[19] Consequent upon this policy and coupled with the demise of several Malay *datu* during the occupation years and in the late 1940s, the traditional Malay aristocratic leadership was greatly eroded.[20] The educated

Malay middle class, which had been expressing dissatisfaction with the traditional leadership since the 1930s, emerged with vitality to struggle with the *datu* for leadership of the community; this struggle was clearly embodied in the cession issue. Members of the educated Malay group established organizations such as the revitalised Persatuan Melayu Sarawak or Malay National Union (MNU), and its affiliates such as the Pergerakan Pemuda Melayu (Malay Youth Movement) and the Barisan Pemuda Sarawak (Sarawak Youth Front), which played active roles in the anti-cession movement.[21]

For the Iban educated elite, the experiences gained during the Japanese period undoubtedly boosted their confidence in their own abilities while at the same time raising their political consciousness. Edward Brandah, a post-war Iban police inspector who did not 'collaborate' with the Japanese regime but joined the SRD, pointed out that affairs relating to the administration of the indigenous peoples 'only require ... 30 per cent' of 'western brains' while 'the rest should be native. The idea came to me as far back as when I was in the interior of Sarawak during the Jap[anese] occupation.'[22]

The core of this group of Kuching-based mission-educated Ibans decided to take a more active role in the political affairs facing the country during the immediate post-war years, namely the debate over cession of Sarawak to Britain. In March 1946, the Sarawak Dayak Association (SDA) was registered as a social organization with its avowed aims including the 'promotion of unity among the various Iban and Land Dayak groups ... their social, moral, educational, and intellectual advancement; [and] the introduction of modern methods of agriculture'.[23] The SDA became involved in the cession controversy through its close links with the MNU and the anti-cession movement.[24]

THE STRAINING OF INTER-ETHNIC RELATIONS

If the British colonial authorities were selective in their treatment of collaborators, the Ibans and other indigenous peoples gave swift retribution to those whom they regarded as collaborators. Besides Japanese companies, Chinese commercial firms were appointed by the military government as agents to oversee the distribution of goods and the system of forced deliveries. Therefore, through the eyes of the natives, these Chinese were collaborators of the Japanese regime and traitors to the Brooke Raj. The brief interregnum (15 August to 11 September 1945) between the Japanese surrender and the arrival of Australian troops witnessed some ugly massacres perpetrated by Ibans on the Chinese. The worst incident occurred in Kanowit where twenty-three Chinese heads were taken.[25] In the aftermath of the Kanowit killings, rumours circulated among the Kuching Chinese community that Ibans from Dutch Borneo had crossed into Serian district and, with their local brethren, were planning to march on Kuching to massacre all Chinese. Meanwhile, an Iban 'reign of terror' enveloped Serian town with the killing of a Malay police constable who was well known for his pro-Japanese sentiments.[26] The rumoured march on Kuching, however, did not materialize. There were also reports of Ibans killing Chinese in the Baram and the Upper Rejang.[27]

Curiously the Chinese backlash came in a series of riots in several towns throughout the country aimed not at Ibans, but at 'punishing' Malays for collaborating with the Japanese. Chinese animosity towards Malays came from witnessing Malay leaders working closely with the Japanese regime, the retention of Malay civil and police personnel at their posts, and the lesser hardship experienced by the Malay community as a whole. The situation in Kuching was particularly grim when a thousand-strong Chinese mob gathered outside the Brooke Dockyard in preparation for a march on the Mosque and Malay villages in the vicinity. Australian troops rushed to the scene and managed to disarm the rioters; and a 24-hour curfew was imposed. It is uncertain how great was the number of casualties during the clash with the soldiers; the figures of Chinese killed ranged from ten to a hundred.[28]

Notwithstanding these unfortunate inter-racial outbursts following the Japanese surrender, there were no other similar incidents reported when civil government was fully restored from mid-April 1946:

> The impact of rising ethnic and political consciousness on communal relations in the early postwar period is difficult to gauge. No evidence exists of any overt tension between groups after the reestablishment of effective government and the waning of the passions of the immediate post-occupation period.[29]

Nevertheless there was underlying tension in Sino-Malay relations. The Chinese community, which had witnessed the 'political awakening' of the Malays during the cession controversy, saw the Malays as a political threat despite the withdrawal of Brooke-style paternalism from the Malays by the British colonial authorities. The Malays, on their part, also felt politically threatened by the Chinese with their heightened nationalism and Leftist leaning politics. Morever in the absence of their special privileges in government service, a 'protective umbrella' had been lifted from the Malays who had now 'to fend for themselves'. Furthermore the numerical superiority of the Chinese, comprising about 27 per cent of the total population (1947) to the Malays' 18 per cent, was naturally disconcerting to the latter.[30]

THE ISSUE OF COLLABORATION AND CHINESE-NATIVE RELATIONS

An outburst of inter-racial hostilities, something not seen in Sarawak since the Bau Chinese march on Kuching in 1857, erupted during the brief interregnum between the Japanese surrender (15 August 1945) and the arrival of Australian troops (11 September 1945). The most serious of these inter-ethnic clashes, namely between Chinese and native races, occurred in Kanowit as mentioned where twenty-three Chinese heads were taken by Iban irregular forces (one of the guerilla bands which were armed, briefly trained and commanded by the Australian SRD). It is uncertain exactly what motivated the Kanowit killings. Those Chinese who were massacred might have been seen by the Ibans as Japanese collaborators and killed as a kind retribution. Arrests were made but, following a long hearing, the Sibu court acquitted the accused, much to the disgust and fury of the Chinese community. The fact that repeated appeals to re-open the case were turned down, further infuriated the Chinese and soured Chinese-Iban relations for a long time in the Rejang.

Following the Kanowit killings, rumours circulated in Kuching that Ibans from Dutch Borneo had crossed the border and, together with their local counterparts, had massed in the Serian district and were planning an invasion of Kuching to massacre the Chinese. Meanwhile an Iban 'reign of terror' was launched in Serian; the only fatality, however, was a Malay policeman, well known to be particularly helpful to the Japanese, who was tied up and shot by the mob. A macabre twist to the horror was the story told of the corpse being dissected and eaten by the killers.[31] The rumoured Iban march on Kuching fortunately did not eventuate, but Chinese fears and paranoia already bordered on hysteria.

However, it must be emphasized that the Kanowit massacre was an isolated case; there were a few killings in the Baram and the Upper Rejang but no other mass killings. 'These incidents', a commentator emphasized, 'were on a small scale, but their psychological repercussions were wide'.[32]

Undoubtedly during the Brooke days, Chinese-native relations had been uneasy particularly in connection with land issues, and Ibans and other natives repeatedly accused the Chinese of encroaching on their communal holdings. Although these land disputes were generally resolved by the Brooke courts, they gave rise to a sense of mistrust on the part of the natives towards the immigrant Chinese. The Ibans, it was pointed out, have 'no great love for the Chinese';[33] the feeling was, however, mutual, for the Chinese had long regarded the Ibans and other natives as uncouth and uncivilized peoples.

Therefore, under wartime circumstances, when each group saw the other as collaborating with the Japanese, it heightened the latent tension between them. The fact that the majority of the SRD recruits in the Baram and Rejang were natives – Kayans, Kenyahs and Ibans – led to isolated incidents of killings of Chinese collaborators, and not, as was the case in Malaya, of Chinese vengeance on native (Malay) collaborators.

The fact that many Malay and Iban police personnel and Native Officers remained at their post and cooperated with the Japanese administration throughout the occupation suggested to the Chinese that natives could not be trusted, and the Chinese were incensed when native collaborators were left unpunished both by the Rajah's government and by the Colonial authorities after they assumed control. In fact, a directive dated 30 March 1946 from the BMA at Labuan to the Liaison Officer, Kuching, declared a general pardon for all collaborators:

> It has been decided by H.M. Government as an act of clemency not to institute further proceedings against persons alleged to be guilty of collaboration with the enemy in British territories of S.E.A. [South-East Asia] where no atrocities or brutality is involved.
>
> This exception however will not cover persons charged with collaboration whose activities as informers directly led to atrocities or brutality or murder by the enemy.
>
> Where convictions have been obtained in the type of case to which His Majesty's Government have now decided to extend clemency, pardon will be granted and the convicted person released.[34]

Incidents such as the Kanowit killings and the trial thereafter were a slap in the face to the Chinese community who had hoped that justice would be done.

The Chinese backlash came in a series of riots in several towns throughout the country. Benedict Sandin, a Saribas Iban who served as a clerk under the Japanese, maintained that the Kanowit killings and fear of an Iban invasion of

Kuching, a reminder of the gory days of 1857 where Ibans hunted Chinese heads following the Bau Chinese defeat, spurred the Chinese into action against the natives, Ibans and Malays alike.[35] In Kuching, for instance, a thousand strong Chinese mob gathered outside the Brooke Dockyard in preparation for a march on the Mosque and the Malay *kampung* beyond. The Chinese accused the Malays of being traitors to the Raj and said that it was time that they (the Malays) were given a beating. Australian troops, however, disarmed the rioters and a 24-hour curfew was imposed. 'While it seems likely that there were no more than ten fatalities,' R. H. W. Reece maintains, 'it is commonly believed in Kuching that as many as 100 Chinese were killed and that the whole affair was hushed up by the military administration for fear of further trouble'.[36]

COLLABORATION AND CHINESE COMMUNAL LEADERSHIP

The real collaborators were men who deliberately joined forces with the enemy and informed on their friends. They were permitted to retain most of their property, they never suffered privation and, in some cases, added to their possessions. Through their tale-bearing, their friends and other loyal persons were tortured, persecuted and killed. I have no sympathy for these collaborators. Owing to the legal difficulties, and for other reasons ... the majority of them were never tried and punished. They are now walking about, free men and, in their own estimation, stainless citizens and pillars of society. Their oleaginous manners and buttery efforts to be well in with the people-who-matter unfortunately deceive the unwary; they are spoken of as such 'good chaps', such 'decent fellows'. The humbler people know better.[37]

If the Chinese could do little to punish native collaborators, there was even less action on their part against their fellow countrymen who sided with the enemy, particularly those so-called *towkay* communal leaders.

The *towkay*, the business leaders and commercial entrepreneurs, had been regarded by the Brooke government as *de facto* leaders and representatives of the Chinese community, the majority comprising peasant farmers, petty traders, artisans and coolies. The counsels of these men were sought by the administration in relation to Chinese affairs. However far from being the voice of the community, these *towkay* leaders were mere wealthy merchants, although they no doubt wielded a certain degree of influence and power on account of their business dealings.[38] These *towkay* comprised members of the Chinese Chamber of Commerce, a Kuching-based mercantile organization which the Brooke administration wrongly regarded as the mouthpiece of the entire Chinese community in the country. In the outstations, the *Kapitan China* and Area Headmen, selected on the basis of their wealth, were officially appointed as leaders of the dialect groups. These men were bazaar shopkeepers, the outstation counterparts of the Kuching, Sibu and Miri *towkay*, with whom they possessed kinship and business ties. Patron-client relationships, clanship structures and occupational specialization along dialect lines reinforced and perpetuated the 'leadership' of the *towkay*.

The *towkay* leaders were generally individuals who, more often than not, did not represent the voice of the Chinese masses. A conspicuous example is the representation of the views and interests of the Hakka dialect group, the largest in the Chinese community. The Hakkas, who comprised a third of the Chinese population, had no voice in the *towkay* leadership which was dominated by Hokkiens and Teochews. Moreover, the rural-based peasant farming community of the Hakkas had nothing in common with the *towkay* leadership of the Hokkien-Teochew urban business elite. On the other hand, the Teochews numbering about 9 per cent of the total Chinese population, had strong representation through the *towkay* leadership which they shared with the Hokkiens.[39]

During the occupation, several of these *towkay*, instead of risking punishment for non-cooperation or suffering discomfort and privation in hiding, took the easy option of collaborating with the Japanese administration. In the process they used their proximity and relationship with the enemy to enrich themselves:

> Those traders who remained [in the towns] were obliged to co-operate to some extent with the Japanese administration and with the trading corporations who came in to conduct monopolies over padi, pepper, timber, and rubber. However, as Japan's position weakened, the scarcity of all kinds of goods provided unprecedented opportunities for profit and much of this was used to purchase land and other property. Accordingly, at the end of the war there were in Kuching and Sibu a number of Chinese businessmen who had not only managed to survive the occupation without discomfort but had in fact substantially improved their material position through judicious purchases of property and produce, such as pepper, on a buyers' market. It was upon these men, who were seen to have waxed fat on the misfortunes of others, that resentment focussed.[40]

The fact that neither the Brooke nor the Colonial government took steps to prosecute these collaborators, traitors in Chinese eyes, placed the Chinese community in an uneasy situation in terms of accepting a 'leadership' which no longer had their respect:

> But the Chinese public seeing that Government still recognises these men, decide reluctantly that they must be accepted. They dare not say a thing against their 'leaders', for fear that the 'leaders' will misrepresent them to the Government with which they are apparently in such close contact.[41]

This passive 'acceptance' of the traditional *towkay* leadership was increasingly eroded when alternative leaders began to emerge in the community during the 1950s. The battle for leadership of the Chinese, between the traditional, wealthy but rather discredited *towkay* incumbents, on the one hand, and the young, radical, and (more often than not) Left-leaning challengers, on the other hand, was fought over the control of the Chinese schools. The 'old' guard sought to maintain the status quo while the 'new' struggled to introduce changes that were aimed at imitating current developments in the mainland.

The tragedy of the leadership struggle lies in the fact that the new aspiring leaders were tainted with the brush of communism and Chinese chauvinism which, as far as the Colonial authorities were concerned, represented subversive elements, and they continued to work through the old leadership. Therefore, the opportunity of ousting the traditional *towkay* leader, who had never truly represented the Chinese and who were tainted by collaborators, was lost.

SARAWAK CHINESE NATIONALISM AND THE EMERGENCE OF LEFTIST ELEMENTS

Chinese nationalism begun to manifest itself following a series of momentous events after the Japanese surrender. Chiang Kai-shek's China became a partner with the victorious Allied powers and this spread pride and patriotism among the Sarawak Chinese as regards their homeland. As a result of lobbying from local Chinese, a Chinese Consulate was established in Kuching in 1948 by the Nationalist Nanking government. Two years earlier, the Kuching Chinese Overseas Club, a pro-KMT organization, was constituted. It had support among the Cantonese and Teochew community.[42]

Following the Japanese capitulation there was a popular belief among the Chinese that China had defeated Japan and that the *Nanyang* (South Seas/South-East Asia) would soon be incorporated as a part of China's territory. In Bau it was reported in early 1946 that 'Some unnamed irresponsible Chinese have been issuing propaganda (verbal) to the DYAKS that the RAJAH's Government is finished, and that CHINA will rule EAST ASIA and the FAR EAST'.[43] The following month brought further pro-China statements:

> The CHINESE are in some cases going so far as to say that SARAWAK should be administered under mandate from CHINA. This idea of making SARAWAK a little CHINA is becoming increasingly prevalent and may well be a contributed [sic contributory] cause to inter-racial trouble in the future.[44]

Lending credence to these rumours was the deployment of Nationalist troops in parts of northern Vietnam in August 1945 following the Japanese demobilization.[45] The civil war that subsequently erupted in China saw the KMT and the CCP both wooing overseas Chinese for allegiance and support. When Mao Tse-tung announced at Tiananmen Square the People's Republic of China (PRC) in 1949, a surge of exaltation swept through the Sarawak Chinese community.[46]

Against this backdrop of events on the mainland, the cession issue, which dominated the political stage of Sarawak during the immediate post-war years, was acted out. The decision of Rajah Vyner to cede his possession to the British Crown sparked Malay opposition. Anti-cessionist demonstrations, speeches, pamphlets and newspapers which stirred Malay political consciousness also indirectly affected the Chinese. The Chinese generally supported cession and the prospect of Colonial Office administration, but the upsurge of Malay nationalism on such an unprecedented scale aroused a political consciousness among the relatively indifferent Chinese.

Subversive elements of the far Left began a campaign to win over the Chinese.[47] A nascent communist movement among the peasant Hakka farming community on the outskirts of Kuching and along the Simanggang Road, with roots dating back to the Japanese period, began to agitate for political action by the Chinese. A report on the First Division for the month of February 1946 made the following remarks:

> The chief cause of concern in KUCHING is the activities of a group of young irresponsible CHINESE. Their politics are

more than slightly flavoured with communism and they seemed to have little or no desire to direct their efforts towards real citizenship. They are mostly immigrants, in most cases well educated in a scholastic sense. They are no doubt in touch with a more rabid communism in SINGA-PORE from whence much of their literature is derived. They are no doubt intimidating Towkays and already looked upon themselves as leading political lights of SARAWAK ... [They are] more concerned with their 'Will-to-power' than for the good of SARAWAK ...

A new Association of CHINESE women is about to be formed ... among their members some of the more polit-ical[ly] minded young women. It is quite expected that this Young Women's Association will link up with the critical movement which has been described above.[48]

This Chinese political awakening came to a head over the *Kuo-yu*[49] controversy and the conversion of Chinese vernacu-lar schools to English during the 1950s. The Colonial Office Administration's plan to use English as the medium of instruction for all subjects in secondary schools provoked opposition from the Chinese community. The arguments against the 'Conversion Plan' centred on the need for the preservation of Chinese language and culture, and the contin-ued practice of education along racial lines which was con-sidered as a means of maintaining Chinese identity.[50]

The effort to preserve communal-based education was fuelled by the desire in certain sectors of the Chinese com-munity to maintain Chinese separateness. The majority of the advocates of this ethnic insularity of the Chinese from the wider Sarawak society were from the Chinese-educated group within the Chinese community who had become increasingly chauvinistic in outlook and assertive of their 'Chineseness' during the post-war years. The gap between the two camps in the Chinese community, namely between the Chinese-educated and the English-educated, had become more pronounced in the post-war years when *Kuo-yu* educa-tion replaced the dialect schools of the Brooke period.[51]

Kuo-yu was wholly unintelligble to the English-educated group. The majority of the English-educated Chinese generally did not support the continuance of education along racial lines for it would further accentuate the differences between themselves and their Chinese-educated brethren. But for the communists, communal schools (and particularly the Chinese Middle Schools) had to be maintained intact at all costs because such institutions provided 'nurseries' from which their members were recruited.[52] Therefore, Leftist elements resisted wholeheartedly the implementation of the 'Conversion Plan' by exploiting the sentiments of the Chinese-educated group for their own ends. However, the communists did not succeed as, by means of persuasion coupled with threats of withdrawing grants-in-aid, the British Colonial government was able to convince the majority of the management committees of Chinese Middle Schools to accept the 'Conversion Plan'.[53] The majority, subsequently, were persuasively won over.

CONCLUSION

'Forgive and forget' seemed to be the policy adopted by postwar administrations in addressing the collaboration issue. Consequently Malay and Chinese communal leadership were retained by the pre-war traditional elite notwithstanding the wartime activities of these individuals. It was indeed a totally unsatisfactory situation but the masses without any alternative influence or channel to the government had grudgingly to accept these communal leaders, amongst whom were clear turncoats. Furthermore, the so-called traditional *towkay* communal leaders of the Chinese were no more than rich merchants who were neither representative of, nor possessed any real interest and understanding of the bulk of the Chinese working-class population. The emergence of a young crop of Chinese leaders during the late 1940s and 1950s tentatively offered a challenge to the entrenched *towkay* elite. However, the Leftist element amongst these 'Young Turks' penalised and prejudiced their leadership contention. The brief flame of the opportunity 'to govern' given to the Iban-educated elite during the occupation was summarily snuffed by the post-war regime. Therefore, like the Malay and Chinese communal leadership, pre-war non-Muslim native leaders retained their pre-eminent position as representatives and spokesmen of their respective communities.

Notes

1.   For MacArthur's plans and alterations, see John Robertson, *Australia at War 1939–1945* (Melbourne: William Heinemann, 1981) pp. 177–8. See also Simon Francis, 'Wartime Intelligence Reports on Borneo', *Borneo Research Bulettin (BRB)*, 25 (1993) 137–41; and D. M. Horner (ed.) *The Commanders: Australian Military Leadership in the twentieth century* (Sydney: George Allen & Unwin, 1984) pp. 202–24.

2.   For the reoccupation of Sarawak, which came under the operation codenamed 'Oboe 6' where the AIF 9th Division landed at the Brunei Bay area and Labuan, see Gary Waters, 'The Labuan Island & Brunei Bay Operation', in *Australian Army Amphibious Operations in the South-West Pacific: 1942–45*, ed. Gleen Wahlert (Papers of the Australian Army History Conference held at the Australian War Memorial, 15 November 1994, Canberra: Australian Army Doctrine Centre, 1995) pp. 71–102; C. Huggett, 'The Borneo Campaign', in *Bayonets Abroad: A History of the 2/13 Battalion A.I.F. in the Second World War*, ed. G. J. Gearnside (Swanbourne, W. Australia: John Burridge, 1993) pp. 383–406; David Horner, *The Gunners: A History of Australian Artillery* (St Leonards, N.S.W.: Allen and Unwin, 1995) pp. 415–17; Gavin Long, *The Final Campaigns* (Canberra: Australian War Memorial, 1963) pp. 453–71; Robertson, *Australia at War*, pp. 178–81; George Odgers, *Air War Against Japan* (Canberra: Australian War Memorial, 1957) pp. 462–79; G. Hermon Gill, *Royal Australian Navy* (Canberra: Australian War Memorial, 1968) pp. 636–45; Peter Donovan, *Waltzing Matildas: The Men and Machines of the 2/9th Australian Armoured Regimental Group in Australia and Borneo 1941–1946* (Blackwood, S. Australia: Donovan and Associates, 1988) pp. 146–72; Bruce Trebeck et al. (ed.), *'What We Have ... We Hold! A History of the 2/17 Australian Infantry Battalion 1940–1945* (Balgowlah, N.S.W.:

2/17 Battalion History Committee, 1998) pp. 295–308; Ken Harvey-Ward, *The Sappers' War with Ninth Australian Division Engineers 1939–1945* (Neutral Bay, N.S.W.: Sakoga in conjunction with 9th Division RAE Association, 1992) pp. 152–55, 163–80; and Ronald J. Austin, *Let Enemies Beware! 'Caveant Hostes': The History of the 2/15th Battalion, 1940–1945* (McCrae: 2/15th Battalion AIF, Remembrance Club Inc., 1995) pp. 267–94. See also Peter Stanley, ' "Sniffing the ground": Australians and Borneo – 1945, 1994', *Journal of the Australian War Memorial (JAWM)*, 25 (October 1994) 32, 37–43.

3. In early 1945, SRD units were parachuted behind enemy lines in central and north-east Borneo to organize resistance in preparation for Allied landings. Most of the SRD personnel were Australians with a fair number of British and New Zealand servicemen. Local recruits were initially from amongst the Kayans, Kenyahs and Muruts including some Chinese from Sarawak's Fourth and Fifth Divisions; later Ibans from the Rejang also joined in the fight. For the background to SRD, see Alan Powell, *War by Stealth: Australians and the Allied Intelligence Bureau 1942–1945* (Melbourne: Melbourne University Press, 1996) pp. 1–31.

4. For instance, *Semut 1*, under the command of Major Tom Harrisson, accounted for 'over 1000 Japanese killed' out of the 'Z' total of 1700.

    Harrisson (who after the War, became the Government Ethnologist and Curator of the Sarawak Museum) wrote a lively account of *Semut* Operation. See Tom Harrisson, *World Within: A Borneo Story* (London: The Cresset Press, 1959). Chong Ah Onn, one of Harrisson's many Chinese 'flitters', recorded his involvement in assisting *Semut* activities in a series of articles published in the *SG*. See Chong Ah Onn, '1943–46, Fifth Division, Sarawak – Part I', *SG*, 29 November 1952, pp. 263–5; Part II, *SG*, 31 December 1952, pp. 283–7; and Part III, *SG*, 30 January 1953, pp. 11–13.

    The most recent account of *Semut* Operation is Bob Long *Operation Semut 1:'Z' Special Unit's Secret War; Soldiering with the Head-Hunters of Borneo* (Maryborough, Victoria: Australian Print Group, 1989). It is a compilation of the recollections of Australian and New Zealand operatives regarding their experiences. For a more thorough critical treatment of SRD *Semut* operations, see Powell, *War by Stealth*, pp. 283–307.

5. The last Japanese unit to surrender was the Fujino force, which had retreated into the Ulu Trusan and continued the struggle until 8 November 1945.

6. After the fall of Singapore, 2750 Allied POWs were trans-
ported to Sandakan for imprisonment. Out of this number
2000 were Australians of the AIF 8th Division, and 750
British soldiers from various units including the RAF, Royal
Artilley (RA), Argyll and Sutherland and Gordon Highlanders,
29th Motor Transport Royal Australian Service Corps (RASC),
Loyals and Royals, and a few Malayan volunteers. See Ivor
M. Purden 'Japanese P.O.W. Camps in Borneo', in *Borneo: The
Japanese P.O.W. Camps – Mail of the Forces, P.O.W. and
Internees*, Neville Watterson (Wellingborough: W. N. Watterson,
1989) p. 23:

> Until September 1944 only 120 had died, but thereafter
> bashings and malnutrition caused a sharp rise in the death
> rate. The Australians in Borneo suffered the fate feared by
> prisoners in other camps – mass killings by Japanese guards
> as defeat approached. To help kill the Australians the
> Japanese withheld medical supplies, and in January 1945
> began to force weakened men to make death marches.
> Many were shot. Of the 2000 Australians, together with 500
> British prisoners in the same camps, only six lived through
> the ordeal.

All the six survivors were Australians who managed to escape.
Robertson, *Australia at War*, p. 207. For a detailed account of
this tragedy, see Hank Nelson, *P.O.W. Prisoners of War:
Australians under Nippon* (Sydney: Australian Broadcasting
Corporation, 1985) pp. 98–124; Don Wall, *Kill the Prisoners*
(Sydney: D. Wall, 1996); Charlie Johnstone, *To Sandakan: the
diaries of Charlie Johnstone, prisoner of war 1942–45* (St
Leonards, N.S.W.: Allen & Unwin, 1995); and Patsy Adam-
Smith, *Prisoners of War: From Gallipoli to Korea* (Ringwood,
Victoria: Viking/Penguin Books Australia, 1992) pp. 365–95.
  See also Athol Randolph Moffitt, *Project Kingfisher* (Sydney:
Angus & Robertson, 1989). This is a version from the view-
point of one of the prosecuting counsel in the war crimes
trials held at Labuan shortly after the war.

7. Apparently, there was also a pre-arranged plan whereby
the civilian internees and POWs of Batu Lintang were to be
eliminated:

> In a detailed order for the day, all people in captivity were
> placed in one of four categories and were to be "liqui-
> dated" in the following manner: –
>
> *Group 1.* Women internees, children and nuns – to be given
> poisoned rice – arrangements under Doctor Yamamoto.

> *Group 2.* Internee men and Catholic Fathers to be shot and burnt under the direction of Lieutenant Ogema.
> *Group 3.* 500 British – American – Dutch and Australian P.O.W's to be marched by Lieutenant Nekata to the mountains on Sarawak–Dutch border carrying all Japanese kit and stores twenty-one miles. On concluding the march all were to be shot and burnt deep in the jungle. (Work had already begun on the pit designed to hide the bodies.)
> *Group 4.* The sick and weak left at Lintang Main Camp to be bayoneted and the entire camp destroyed by fire.

Papers of L. E. Morris (91/18/1, IWM). Morris recorded this in his diary dated 10 October 1945; he was convinced that this macabre and dastardly plan was intended to be implemented by Suga on 15 September. 'It has now been established beyond all doubt', wrote Morris in his diary entry of 10 October, 'that Suga intended to "dispose" of all prisoners on September 15th'.

The so-called 'Death' directive was apparently found in the Administration Office of Batu Lintang. Furthermore Morris alledged that higher authorities had approved 'the plan as a matter of policy'.

However, according to a civilian internee this 'death' directive originated 'from Japanese High Command' and not from the Camp Commandant Lieutenant Colonel Suga himself, as is implied in Morris's version. Moreover, Bates believed that Suga apparently disregarded the directive. Bates recorded these observations in her journal entry dated 7 August 1945, two months prior to Morris's account. See Papers of Miss H. E. Bates (MSS 91/35/1, IWM) pp. 118–19. See also '[Prisoners of War and Internees:] Report of investigations of the fate of Allied POW and Internees in British Borneo (namely British North Borneo, Labuan, Brunei and Sarawak). Compiled by Capt L. G. Darling, 9th Australian Division (August–December 1945), AWM54 779/1/25 (AWMA).

8. 'Autobiography of C. F. C. Macaskie', Papers of C. F. C. Macaskie (MSS Pac s. 71, RHL) p. 132.
9. *Sarawak Annual Report 1947* (Kuching: Government Printing Office, 1948) p. 3.
10. For the work and activities of the BMA, see F. S. V. Donnison, *British Military Administration in the Far East* (London: HMSO, 1956) pp. 188–96.
11. Cited in 'Autobiography', Papers of C. F. C. Macaskie, p. 138.
12. For a detailed study of the end of Brooke rule, see R. H. W. Reece, *The Name of Brooke: The End of White Rajah Rule in Sarawak* (Kuala Lumpur: Oxford University Press, 1982); and

Colin N. Crisswell, *The End of the Brooke Raj in Sarawak* (Kiscadale Asia Research Series No. 1, Gartmore, Stirlingshire: Paul Strachan-Kiscadale, 1994).

13. K. H. Digby, *Lawyer in the Wilderness* (Cornell University Southeast Asia Program Data Paper No. 114, Ithaca, New York: Cornell University Press, October 1980) p. 76.

14. Vyner Brooke to Bertram Brooke, May 1946 (Brooke Papers, MSS Pac. s. 83, Box 19, RHL).

15. Digby, *Lawyer in the Wilderness*, p. 76.

16. Ibid.

17. 'S.O.I. Legal to Liaison Officer, Kuching, 23 April 1946' (WO 203/5991, PRO).

18. Reece, *Name of Brooke*, p. 147. For the treatment of Bay and Insol by the British Colonial government, see pp. 153–5.

19. Towards the closing days of Brooke rule, the ethnic composition of the civil service comprised: 1371 Malays; 456 non-Malay natives (mostly Ibans); 426 Chinese; and 49 Europeans. Michael B. Leigh, *The Rising Moon: Political Change in Sarawak* (Sydney: Sydney University Press, 1974) p. 23.

20. Out of the eight Kuching *datu*, two passed away during the occupation. Several others died in the mid- or late 1940s. In fact, the 1950s only witnessed two *datu* who were active, namely the *Hakim* and the *Bandar*. The Datu Hakim Haji Mohidin was the leading authority on *adat* and Islamic jurisprudence. He died in 1957. The Datu Bandar Abang Haji Mustapha, formerly the *datu pahlawan*, was elevated to this exalted position after the war; a deserving promotion as a reward for his strong and active support of cession. His pro-Japanese and anti-British stance during the occupation was quietly and hastily swept under the carpet. The Datu Bandar Abang Haji Mustapha was the chief advisor to the British Colonial government on Malay affairs. See C. A. Lockard, *From Kampung to City: A Social History of Kuching, Malaysia, 1820–1970* (Ohio University Monographs in International, Studies Southeast Asia Series, No. 75, Athens, Ohio: Ohio University Press, 1987) pp. 158–9.

21. See Reece, *Name of Brooke*, pp. 246–78; and Sanib Said, *Malay Politics in Sarawak 1946–1966: The Search for Unity and Political Ascendancy* (Singapore: Oxford University Press, 1985) *passim*. See also Vernon L. Porritt, *British Colonial Rule in Sarawak 1946–1963* (Kuala Lumpur: Oxford University Press, 1997) pp. 52–57.

22. Edward Brandah to Anthony Brooke, 26 October 1946 (Brooke Papers, MSS Pac. s. 83, Box 13/1, RHL).

23. *Rules and By-Laws of the Dayak Association of Sarawak. Established 1st March 1946, Kuching, 1946*, cited in Reece, *Name of Brooke*, p. 248.

24. See Reece, *Name of Brooke*, pp. 246–78; Lockard, *Kampung to City*, pp. 210, 247–9; and Porritt, *British Colonial Rule in Sarawak*, p. 56.

25. For the Kanowit killings, see 'Annual Report of the District Officer, Kanowit, for the year 1946', Typescript (SMA); and Edwards and P. W. Steven, *Short Histories of the Lawas and Kanowit Districts* (Kuching: Borneo Literature Bureau, 1971), p. 164. Reece maintains that the killings at Kanowit, and also at Song, were the result of 'the encouragement given Ibans [by SRD] to take Japanese heads' which 'got out of control'. See Reece, *Name of Brooke*, p. 150.

26. See Digby, *Lawyer in the Wilderness*, pp. 76–7.

27. See Tom Harrisson, 'The Chinese in Borneo 1942–1946', *International Affairs* (*IA*), 26, 3 (July 1950) p. 360.

28. See Reece, *Name of Brooke*, p. 159.

29. Lockard, *Kampung to City*, p. 180.

30. J. L. Noakes, *Sarawak and Brunei: A Report on the 1947 Population Census* (Kuching: Government Printing Office, 1950) p. 38.

31. See Digby, *Lawyer in the Wilderness*, pp. 76–7. Although it is difficult to substantiate this gory account, another reported case of Iban cannibalism during the liberation of Kapit might perhaps lend support to the credibility of such tales:

> Two Japanese soldiers had hidden themselves in a hole, and were undetected until one made the fatal mistake of shooting at a woman. Discovering them, the Iban were at the hole in seconds, but could not get to the Japanese. Casting caution aside, Penghulu Nyanggau, Temenggong Jinggut's brother, leapt into the hole and was speared by the Japanese. Other Iban got rolls of palm thatch which they lit and threw into the hole. Forced out by the smoke, the Japanese were quickly killed.
>
> Cannibalism is abhorrent to the Iban, but so intense was their hatred for the man who had killed Nyanggau that they cut out his liver and ate it. 'It's true', recalls Tedong [anak Barieng], 'we gutted him. I was with those who ate his liver. The Japanese who killed Nyanggau was the one we did this to.' V. H. Sutlive, *Jr, Tun Jugah of Sarawak: Colonialism and Iban Response* (Kuala Lumpur: Penerbit Fajar Bakti for Sarawak Literary Society, 1992) p. 113.

32. Harrisson, 'The Chinese in Borneo', p. 360.

33.   See Ian Morrisson, 'Local Self-Government in Sarawak', *Pacific Affairs* (*PA*), 22, 2 (June 1949) p. 178.
34.   'S.O.I. Legal to Liaison Officer, Kuching, 23 April 1946' (WO 203/5991, PRO).
35.   Benedict Sandin, unpublished MS, cited in Reece, *Name of Brooke*, p. 152.
36.   Reece, *Name of Brooke*, p. 159.
37.   'Autobiography', J. B. Archer, former Chief Secretary of the Brooke government (1939–1941), cited in T'ien Ju-K'ang, *The Chinese of Sarawak: A Study of Social Structure* (Monograph on Social Anthropology No. 12, London: Department of Anthropology, London School of Economics and Political Science, 1953) p. 76.
38.   For details of Chinese leadership structure in Sarawak, see T'ien, *Chinese of Sarawak*, pp. 68–79; and Craig A. Lockard, 'Leadership and Power Within the Chinese Community of Sarawak: An Historical Survey', *JSEAS*, 2, 2 (September 1971) 195–217.
39.   The percentage of the total Chinese population of the different dialect groups according to the 1947 population census is as follows: Hakka (31.3), Foochow (28.9), Hokkien (14.0), Cantonese (10.1), Teochew (8.9), Henghua (3.0), Hainanese (2.6) and others (1.2). Noakes, *Sarawak and Brunei* p. 93.
40.   Reece, *Name of Brooke*, pp. 156–7.
41.   T'ien, *Chinese of Sarawak*, p. 77.
42.   See *ST*, 27 June 1946; *ST*, 28 April, 9 and 28 August 1947; *ST*, 20 January 1948; *SG*, 1 September 1947, p. 162; *SG*, 2 February 1948, p. 32; Lockard, *Kampung to City*, p. 169; and T'ien p. 86. The KMT-backed Chinese Consulate officially closed on 7 January 1950. See *ST*, 9 January 1950.
43.   'Monthly Report for the Month of January, 1946' (WO 203/5983, PRO).
44.   'First Division: Monthly Report for February, 1946' (WO 203/5983, PRO). See also 'Monthly Report for March 1946 for the Kuching District' (WO 203/5983, PRO).
45.   See Victor Purcell, *The Chinese in Malaya* (Kuala Lumpur: Oxford University Press, 1967) pp. 263–4.
46.   See Lockard, *Kampung to City*, pp. 169–70.
47.   For the development of communism in Sarawak, see Sarawak Information Service, *The Danger Within: A History of the Clandestine Communist Organization in Sarawak* (Kuching: Government Printing Press, 1963), pp. 2–4; *SG*, 30 September 1952, pp. 203–4; Justus M. Van Der Kroef, 'Communism and Chinese Communalism in Sarawak', *The China Quarterly* (*CQ*), 20 (October–December 1964) 38–66, and 'Communism

in Sarawak Today', *Asian Survey (AS)*, 6, 10 (October 1956) 568–79.

48. 'First Division: Monthly Report for February, 1946' (WO 203/5983, PRO).
49. *Kuo-yu* is the vernacular form of Chinese, a simplified version of the classical Chinese language which was introduced in the mainland after the May Fourth Movement in 1919. The introduction of *Kuo-yu* marked a revolution in the Chinese language which enabled a larger proportion of the masses to acquire a rudimentary literacy in the language which was once the preserve of the scholar-bureaucrat ruling elite.
50. See Ooi Keat Gin, 'Education in Sarawak During the Period of Colonial Administration, 1946–1963', *Journal of the Malaysian Branch Royal Asiatic Society (JMBRAS)*, 63, 2 (December 1990) 57–60.
51. For the development of Chinese education during the Brooke period, see Ooi Keat Gin, 'Chinese Vernacular Education in Sarawak During Brooke Rule, 1841–1946', *Modern Asian Studies (MAS)*, 28, 3 (July 1994) 503–31.
52. See *The Danger Within*, p. 25.
53. See Ooi, 'Education in Sarawak, 1946–1963', pp. 59–60; and Porritt, *British Colonial Rule in Sarawak*, pp. 82–83.

Conclusion

Like their compatriots in other South-East Asian countries, the inhabitants of Sarawak experienced privation as a result of the occupation and the Pacific War, but the territory faced comparatively fewer and lesser hardships than other similarly occupied lands in the region. There was little physical damage to buildings or loss of property, and atrocities were relatively uncommon. Several Malay leaders in Kuching and young educated Ibans in the Second Division were favoured by the Japanese *Gunseibu*. A young Mission-educated Iban, Eliab Bay, was appointed liaison officer on Iban affairs to the Japanese military at Simanggang. Many Malay policemen were swiftly promoted in rank; Ibans, hitherto few in number in the police force, were urged to join, and several received rapid promotion. Generally the Kuching and Sibu Chinese *towkay* communal leaders and bazaar shopkeepers in the out-stations cooperated with the Japanese; few were enthusiastic, but none was overtly opposed. Sarawak did not have any active anti-Japanese underground movements such as the Malayan Peoples' Anti-Japanese Army (MPAJA) of Malaya or Chinese-led guerilla organizations such as the group that launched the ill-fated 'Double-Tenth' in Jesselton, former British North Borneo, in 1943.

For most of the Japanese occupation period, the majority of the native population generally led a normal existence centred on a subsistence-based livelihood. There was obviously a scarcity of goods in the bazaar and no market for rubber which the natives used to sell for cash. In the upriver and hilly districts of the interior, native inhabitants hardly had the opportunity to meet any Japanese face to face. When the food shortage situation became acute from mid-1944 and the campaign for food self-sufficiency was intensified, some of the native longhouses in the interior had to sell their surplus rice stocks to government-appointed agents, mostly local Chinese bazaar shopkeepers. Certain groups of long-houses and villages were instructed to contribute labour gangs for work in airfields and other projects; some young men were recruited to serve in logging camps and as sawmill workers. Many returned with tales of hard work and stinging slaps received from their Japanese overseers.

Some native young men, probably encouraged by a Native Officer and also motivated by their own sense of *bejalai* instinct of adventure, applied to participate in a Japanese-sponsored training programme, *kyodotai*. The harshness of their Japanese trainers, the difficulty in communication, and rumours of an imminent Japanese defeat created disillusion-ment among these young men; consequently many deserted to return home while others decided to join bands of Australian SRD operatives and their local allies of Kayans, Kenyahs and Muruts in fighting the Japanese.

Many longhouse communities, despite the order to report on anti-Japanese activities to the local authorities, decided to disregard such instructions. Instead, when armed Australian soldiers sought their assistance, they readily offered the sol-diers their hospitality and protection, and even joined them in attacking Japanese outposts. Likewise, downed American airmen were given assistance and protection.

Many Ibans were infuriated when the Japanese com-manded them to surrender their hunting rifles. Those who resisted were severely punished. Iban hatred for the Japanese increased and those who were associated with them, like certain Chinese shopkeepers and Malay policemen, were targeted for retribution when the opportunity arose.

Some village Malay and Chinese schools organized classes to teach the Japanese language, imitating their urban coun-terparts. Native children and adults alike picked up some *Nippon-go* words and phrases, sang some songs without com-prehending the meaning of the lyrics, and bowed to a picture of the Japanese 'Rajah'. None of these activities meant anything; many awaited the return of their 'White Tuan' whom, some unknowingly thought, were on a rather extended furlough.

In towns such as Kuching, Sibu and Miri, and the other smaller urban centres, the Malay community had little to complain of. The big Chinese shops which many thought would never be without provisions surprisingly ran out of stocks. The shortage of textiles meant that aristocratic Malay womenfolk had to dispense with their veil to save cloth. The Malays also witnessed the sudden 'disappearance' of Chinese into the countryside. As for themselves, those who were farmers and fishermen continued with their livelihoods, as did their neighbours who served in government service and in the police force. Those in the administration as Native Officers continued with their work; instead of answering to a European superior, they had a Japanese instead. Those in the police force remained as before; some of their colleagues were promoted.

Occasionally there were public gatherings where school children sang and cultural dances were performed, and community leaders gave speeches. Some of these speakers attacked Britain and America and praised Japan, while others diplomatically avoided commitment to either side. The Japanese authorities distributed leaflets to the public, few, however, understood what it meant because the majority could not read the romanized Malay or Iban characters.

The foregoing scenario of the experiences of indigenous communities during the occupation demonstrate that the Japanese period did not to a great extent benefit the indigenous people of Sarawak, but neither did it adversely affect them. No doubt some native individuals did profit from the experiences gained during this time while others suffered, but the fact remains that the majority of the indigenous peoples were little affected by the various Japanese policies.

The Chinese community in Sarawak survived the difficult years of the Japanese occupation without significant changes. The Chinese continued to control the country's economy as during the pre-war days. The limited physical damage to the country's infrastruture meant that commercial activities could be restored as soon as shipping and communication facilities became available with Singapore, the country's major trading partner. The period of rehabilitation was brief and, by the late 1940s and early 1950s, Chinese businesses were on the road to full recovery.

Notwithstanding the charges of collaboration, the traditional *towkay* leadership retained its position and continued to dominate the power structure within the community. The emergence of an alternative leadership composed of younger, more radical, and generally Leftist men, was shrugged off by the old guard. The challenge to their leadership by the Leftists, in fact, further strengthened the position of these traditional leaders, who had the support of the Colonial government.

The continuation of the traditional elite leadership could be seen when political parties were established during the late 1950s. For instance, Ong Kee Hui, a founding leader of the Sarawak United People's Party (SUPP), the first political party in the country, was the grandson of the Hokkien *Kapitan China* General, Ong Tiang Swee, the most important Chinese leader during the reigns of Rajah Charles and Rajah Vyner. If SUPP was the stronghold of the traditional Hokkien elite, than the Sarawak Chinese Association (SCA) was the organ of the Kuching Teochew and the Sibu Foochow traditional commercial leadership. William Tan, the SCA's first president, like Ong, came from a wealthy background and was himself a successful businessman.[1]

Although it cannot be denied that Chinese nationalism and political consciousness had been aroused to a degree not witnessed during pre-war years, political developments in Sarawak (and particularly in China) had, even more than the Japanese interregnum, been responsible. The cession controversy had demonstrated the political consciousness of the Malays; the Chinese, having witnessed this Malay awakening, began to realize their own political interests and rights. The emergence of Mao's China fed hopes among the Sarawak Chinese of a rejuvenated motherland. These developments of the late 1940s to a certain extent ignited the flame of political awareness within the hitherto politically inert Chinese community; subsequent events during the 1950s testified to this awakening.

Nevertheless, when Leftist elements with pro-China loyalties and patriotism began to agitate among the Chinese community (and in effect, sought to provide an alternative to the traditional *towkay* leadership), they were rejected by the majority of the Sarawak Chinese. The rejection of the Left owed as much to their radicalism and militant posture as to the nature of Sarawak Chinese society. Although there were attempts to lessen speech group particularism by establishing pan-dialect organizations and the introduction of *Kuo-yu* in Chinese schools, dialect loyalties remained strong. The continuity of the *towkay* leadership drawn from the traditional elite of Hokkiens and Teochews demonstrates that dialect particularism remained influential. The Chinese Left, whose supporters came largely from the Hakka peasantry, had difficulty in overcoming the dialect division and was therefore unable to garner support from other speech groups.

But as far as the Chinese community in Sarawak was concerned, the Japanese occupation represented a period of material discomfort and privation without bringing forth any significant transformation.

Three years and eight months of life behind barbed wires affected adversely the health and physical conditions of civilian internees of Batu Lintang. However the majority of fatalities and deaths were amongst the POWs. A considerable number of civilian survivors were Brooke and North Borneo officers of whom, after a period of recuperation in Australia, New Zealand or England, returned to serve in their former capacity, and several joined the British Colonial government after its takeover of Sarawak following cession.

Whatever Japanese anti-Western propaganda that was disseminated amongst Sarawak's inhabitants, it was apparent there were no strong influence and effects on the various communities as can be witnessed during the post-war years. Despite their defeat, flight and capture, and incarceration by the Japanese during the occupation, Brooke officers who returned to their official positions after the war were still highly regarded and respected by the local inhabitants. There were no incidents of insubordination.

The quick succession of governments after the Japanese surrender beginning with a brief period of military rule under the Australians, BMA, and the return of Rajah Vyner's government were smooth transitions. The efficiency of returning to normalcy and civilian rule in large measure boosted European capabilities, which, was never in doubt, in the eyes of the local population. There were hardly any anti-Western sentiments expressed towards Europeans among the various communities. The controversial cession issue also did not sparked anti-Western feelings amongst Malays who rallied to the anti-cession banner. On the contrary in fact the anti-cessionists struggled for the perpetuation of Brooke rule. Such fervent pro-Brooke sentiments reflected their high regard for the Brooke Raj in spite of the failure of Rajah Vyner's government in defending the country and its people against the Japanese onslaught. This pro-Western sentiment was apparent as exhibited during the occupation when indigenous peoples actively assisted SRD operations behind enemy lines.

Therefore, as far as Sarawak was concerned Western prestige remained intact and Europeans who return enjoyed their pre-war status and respect. There was no love lost for the Japanese, whether in victory or in defeat, by the peoples of Sarawak.

TRANSFORMATION OR CONTINUITY?

In terms of the impact of the Japanese occupation on political leadership, some viewed the developments during the brief period as 'catalytic agents in the dissolution of the old order'[2] and, 'as a catalyst ... [in] the last stage of foreign domination'[3] of the countries of South-East Asia. Willard Elsbree and Harry J. Benda, who studied developments in Indonesia (and particularly Benda), argued that the Japanese interregnum was crucial in the emergence of new political elites. This transformation thesis and birth of new elites was closely identified with Benda, and it won the support of other historians.[4] However, a reassessment by a group of scholars during the late 1970s meant they were less convinced of, and subsequently challenged, the claims of the transformation argument and the 'new elites' thesis. Instead, Robert H. Taylor on Burma, David G. Marr on Vietnam and Alfred W. McCoy on the Philippines[5] brought forth the 'elite continuity' thesis; each from their respective country analysis argued that 'the political elites which emerged from the war years were already influential in the pre-war decade'.[6] They further demonstrated 'that what appears, in the narrow context of the 1942–45 period, to be new political leadership was in reality the response of distinct social groups to changed political circumstance, creating the illusion but not the substance of change'.[7] In Malaya and Thailand, it was argued that the pre-war entrenched elites survived and continued to wield power during the post-war period.[8]

A brief overview of Sarawak's situation favoured the 'elite continuity' thesis. Post-war developments witnessed few changes in the faces of the Malay political elite or in the Chinese leadership line-up. Likewise, the traditional Iban leaders and other indigenous chieftains remained pre-eminent as communal leaders.[9] Conspicuously absent were young educated Iban upstarts, those that had enjoyed brief Japanese patronage during the occupation, in the grounds of the Astana for afternoon tea with Rajah Vyner, or later (after July 1946) with the Governor, Sir Charles Noble Arden-Clarke.

Therefore, if in British Malaya (West Malaysia) and the Netherlands East Indies (Indonesia), 'war was an event of near cataclysmic proportions in its armed violence and political disruption', bringing about 'lasting political consequence', or in Burma and the Philippines 'left little more than a trail of physical destruction, such as might follow in the wake of a natural ... upheaval,'[10] then it can be said that Sarawak did not share the same experience as its neighbours. The Sarawak experience, therefore, is more in line with the views that propounded the 'continuity' thesis rather than the 'transformation' argument.

Notes

1. For Chinese leadership in political parties, see Michael B. Leigh, *The Rising Moon: Political Change in Sarawak* (Sydney: Sydney University Press, 1974) pp. 8–23.
2. Willard Elsbree, *Japan's Role in Southeast Asian Nationalist Movements 1940 to 1945* (New York: Institute of Pacific Relations, 1953) p. 167.
3. Harry J. Benda, *Continuity and Change in Southeast Asia* (New Haven Yale University, Southeast Asia Studies No. 18, 1972) p. 149.
4. See Benedict R. O'G Anderson, 'Japan: "The Light of Asia"'; Dorothy Guyot, 'Burma Independence *Army* A Political Movement in Military Garb'; and David Steinberg, 'The Philippine "Collaborators": Survival of an Oligarchy' in *Southeast Asia in World War II: Four Essays*, ed. Josef Silverstein (New Haven: Yale University, Southeast Asia Studies No. 7, 1966).
5. Robert H. Taylor, 'Burma in the Anti Fascist War'; David G. Marr, 'World War II and the Vietnamese Revolution'; and Alfred W. McCoy, '"Politics By Other Means": World War II in the Western Visayas, Philippines', in *Southeast Asia under Japanese Occupation*, ed. Alfred W. McCoy (New Haven: Yale University, Southeast Asia Studies No. 22, 1980).
6. McCoy, *Southeast Asia under Japanese Occupation*, p. 5.
7. Ibid., p. 6.
8. See Yoji Akashi, 'The Japanese Occupation of Malaya: Interruption or Transformation?'; Cheah Boon Kheng, 'The Social Impact of the Japanese Occupation of Malaya (1942–1945)'; and Benjamin A. Batson, 'Siam and Japan: The Perils of Independence', in McCoy, *Southeast Asia under Japanese Occupation*.
9. See Ooi Keat Gin, 'Japanese Attitudes towards the Indigenous Peoples of Sarawak, 19141–1945', Symposium on the Japanese Occupation in South-East Asia, National University of Singapore, Singapore, 13–17 December 1995.
10. McCoy, *Southeast Asia under Japanese Occupation*, p. 8.

Appendix: A Brief History of Kuching, Dec[ember] [19]41–Sep[tember] [19]45

Chief Informant: KOH SOON EWE, married Chinese, at present employed as clerk by BBCAU. Pre-war was with Civil Administration working under the previous Chief Secretary of Sarawak, Mr [J. Beville] Archer. Forced by Japs to work in Jap civil administration. Recommended to me[1] by Mr Archer for above purpose. Dates are from memory and an approximate only.

19–12–41   15 Jap[2] planes bombed Kuching. Direct hit Borneo Co benzine store. 30 killed. After the bombing bazaars closed and most of the people left Kuching for outer suburbs, jungle and seaside.

24–12–41   Evening Japs landed. Informant left for outer suburbs, but heard shooting for days.

26–12–41   Govt offices re-opened, Banks remained closed until 1944. Early 1942 Yokohama Specie Bank opened.

Jan 42   All motor cars impressed by military, all buses and trucks taken over by the Jap Transport Co and small compensation made.

Jan 42   Labour recruited for aerodrome[3] construction – mainly Dyaks, and forced labour. Extra rations and payment as inducement.

Jan 42   Wireless set sealed by Japs. After the fall of Singapore seals removed. About July 1942, all wireless sets confiscated, a small compensation ($5 per valve) being paid in June 1944.

29–1–42   Kuching bombed by one Dutch plane, fell on a house in India Street near the Power Station.

Jan 42   Most of [the] population returned. All the shops re-opened. Japs used same prices (in beginning) as pre[-]war. In the beginning used Sarawak currency,

125

a few months later Jap invasion currency was introduced.

June 42   Military HQ moved from Miri to Kuching. C-in-C lived at 'Astana' (Rajah's Palace)[.] HQ offices were in previous Govt offices – building with the clock tower opposite concrete ramp. C-in-C killed in plane crash soon after arrival – not known where or how.

" "   Instructions issued to population to officially welcome the C-in-C. The Indian Independence League held a procession. Chinese did NOT.

Early 42   Japs asked people to plant padi (rice) sweet potatoes (krebang) and tapioca. During the first 6 months people mortgaged their properties to finance planting of vegetables[.] Financed by Yokohama Specie bank.

" "   Rubber – Japs began purchasing rubber and damar (from which a very poor lubricating oil was made)[.] Not much rubber brought in as prices were low.

About July 1942   Rubber tapping prohibited except at the DAHAN (European) estate. Not known why, though it may have been due to large stocks already held and perhaps to shipping difficulties.

NISSA SHOKAI (in existence at Kuching pre-war) purchased all rubber on behalf of Jap Govt until tapping prohibited.

Quit rent payable on all land pre-war – was abolished after 1943 on rubber holdings.

7 Jul 42   Anniversary of Jap invasion of China. Chinese forced to hold a procession. Chinese flags were flown with 4 Chinese characters added, translation of which is 'Building up the country by peaceful means'. This addition was by order of the Japs, but apparently was not executed in accordance with their orders as all Chinese and Sarawak flags were confiscated. (Or perhaps it was a ruse to confiscate all flags anyhow).

Jul 42   Believed after above leaders of Chinese community [were] arrested, and imprisoned for about a month. One, KAHN AH CHONG (ex Malaya) was kept in prison for about 2 1/2 years.

After Jul 42   A number of Chinese houses were requisitioned by the Japs for offices and residences.

Jul 42   5 Chinese shot publicly for stealing military stores at the aerodrome. This was the first, and last, public execution.

Aug 42   Chinese leaders released on condition that they formed an association, known as 'Overseas Chinese Association'. This association was used for carrying out Japanese orders, of any kind, the association being responsible for passing on such orders to the Chinese e.g.

(i)   A brothel for Japanese officers had to be opened, staffed by Chinese girls.
(ii)   A 'Defence Fund' of $900 000 had to be raised.

End of 42   Head tax imposed $6.00 per head Chinese[;] Malays and Dyaks 50 cents. From 1943 onwards, abolished.

Jul 42   All wireless sets confiscated.

" "   The pre-war 1st Division and 2nd Division amalgamated for purpose of civil administration and known as Kuching Province.

Early 1943   Work commenced on shipbuilding yards at Sungei Priok. As well as PW's [public works] [coolies], local labour, mainly Malays, recruited for this purpose. Chinese shipbuilders imported from Shanghai and Hong Kong. Inducements to work on this project were increased rations, and payment. About 1500–2000 employed. Operations ceased after the bombing on 25 March 1945.

1943   Lottery introduced. The various communities were allotted a certain percentage to fill. Run quarterly.

Early 1943   KYODOHEI [KYODOTAI] (native troops) formed and recruitment for training began. Some were ex-Sarawak [R]angers, Malays and Dyaks. This was a separate force from the police.

Early 1943   JIKEIDAN ('Self Protection Corps') formed. This was a kind of ARP organisation, but it also served to assist the Police in many ways e.g. night patrolling, taking of census etc.

Dec 1943	An Advisory Council KEN SANJI appointed by the Civil Governor. This consisted of about 17 members [comprising all nationalities].
Early 1944	The Southern Development Bank (military) was opened and transacted all Govt business.
Early 44	Shipbuilding and Seamanship training schools opened and was compulsory for those unemployed aged about 16 to 25 years, to attend. They received free food and a small wage. The shipbuilding school was conducted in a new building, completed by the Japs, situated in the Race course grounds. This building was paid for out of Sarawak Jubilee funds.
Apr 44	Jap HQ moved to Jesselton but requisitioned house still retained for Japanese use – especially for the Air Force whose members, including army, had increased. After the bombing of Kuching in March 45 more houses were requisitioned this time Malay houses, as these were less likely to be attacked than the European and better Chinese buildings.
end of 44	The three Chinese banks KWONG LEE (Kuching)[,] BIAN CHIANG (Kuching) and WAT TAT (Sibu), which had been closed since Jan 42, were forced to amalgamate and re-open as the KYOIE Bank ('work together for prosperity').
Dec 44	Rice rations to general public stopped. Only Government employees and employees of Jap companies received a small ration for themselves and families. Government employees received 8 katis (1 kati = 1 1/3 lbs.) male, 5 katis – female[,] 4 katis children, per head per month.
25–3–45	Kuching bombed.
7–9–45	Aust[ralian] medical personnel arrived Kuching by Catalina.
11–9–45	Major General YAMAMURA surrendered on board HMAS 'KAPUNDA' at PENDING to Comd [Commander] Kuching Force (Brigadier EASTICK DSO., ED.) Recce [rescue] party proceeded by road to POW barracks [Batu Lintang] Kuching.
12–9–45	All Jap guards relieved and complete control of Kuching effected. Force HQ established Government Land Office.

16–9–45   Force HQ moved to 'ASTANA' (Rajah's palace).

12–9–45   Evacuation of ALLIED POW's and civil internees to LABUAN commenced. All Jap forces, except a small Liaison HQ in Kuching, being concentrated at BAU from this and adjacent area.

ECONOMIC
Food Supply:

When Japs arrived there were plentiful stocks of rice on hand. The ration system for rice, sugar and salt which was brought into force in 1939/40, was continued by the Japs for the duration. Beginning in 1943 imported foodstuffs such as rice, salt and sugar began to get scarce and the ration scale was steadily reduced. During 1944 the number of shops allowed to remain open was reduced in order that the population should become self-supporting.

The rations of rice to general public ceased in December 44.

Mining:

Goldmining ceased after the arrival of the Japs except for a very small amount. The machinery was removed by the Japs for use at the shipbuilding yards and aerodrome.

Coalmine: Apparently unsuccessful attempts were made to re-open the coal-mine at SADONG.

Mercury: was obtained by the Japs from mines at TEGORA and GADING, employing several hundred coolies (mainly drawn from the goldfields area) from early 42 to Aug 45.

Japanese Business Monopolies:

Jap companies were given monopolies over matches, coconut oil [,] salt and nipa sugar ([later] fish – through the Chinese Fishermen[']s Association.)

SUNDRY ITEMS
Civil Administration:

Only Malays and Dyaks appointed as native District Officers and A[sst]. DO's. As previously stated an Advisory Council ('KEN SANJI') of 17 persons (Kuching area) all races represented, was formed by the Civil Governor in Dec 43.

Schools:

Malay and Chinese schools re-opened in July after 6 months 'recess' using Japanese text books. Japanese language taught in schools and study of Jap language was compulsory for Jap Govt Civil Servants. However, it appears that a policy of passive resistance was used and my informant stated that attendances were poor and very few could speak Japanese.

The Malay language was the official language (after the Japanese).

Medical:

More than 50% of the hospital space was used for the Jap military. Civilians received medical treatment but medical supplies were short. Some quinine was sold by a Jap medicine shop.

Religion:

Chinese temples, Malay and Indian Mosque (Mahommedan), Indian Temple (Hindu) and RC [Roman Catholic] Church were not molested. Only the Church of England and 7th Day Adventist desecrated.

Cinemas:

At first the Japs showed some old pre-war American films. Frequent picture shows beginning 1943 – mainly news propaganda and old pre-war Chinese films. Very few musicals.

Police:

After the Jap landing the police carried on as usual my informant states. He also says that persons arrested were ill-treated by the Indian police.

Indians:

KOH SOON EWE did not know if the India[n] Independence League (as such) existed pre-war, but says it became active upon Jap occupation. The India[n] Moslem Movement (in existence pre-war) was forced to join I.I.L. [India[n] Independence League] later on, date uncertain, possibly in 1943. Frequent processions, at least once per month, Jan 42 to about Aug 44 were held by the India[n] Independence League.

Museum:

The museum remains intact. Translation[s] in Japanese characters were added to a number of exhibits. Some volumes dealing with Borneo were removed.

Library:

Technical books, mainly dealing with Borneo, were removed, but some 6 to 7000 books remain intact and in good condition.

New Construction:

Apart from shipbuilding [and aerodrome] the only new construction appears to be

1. Building on Racecourse of brick and cement.
2. A building, 2 storey, cement, blocking India Street and joining the Treasury and Land Office buildings.
3. Cement swimming pool adjacent to the museum, dimensions approx 17 yards × 28 yards.

Source: Order of battle including location, strength, disposition and movements of units and formations, Mar–Oct 1945 – Borneo (WO 208/1054, PRO).

Notes

1. Author of report is unknown. A hand-scribbled note on the last page of this 4-page report suggests a copy is given to BBCAU, Kuching.
2. 'Jap' denotes 'Japanese' throughout this report.
3. 'Aerodrome' here refers to the 7th Mile Bukit Stabar Landing Ground situated to the south of Kuching town.

References

PRIMARY SOURCES

Imperial War Museum Archives, London

Papers of Miss H. E. Bates, MSS 91/35/1.
Papers of L. E. Morris, 91/18/1.
Papers of E. R. Pepler, 88/33/1.
Papers of G. W. Pringle.
'Borneo Operations 1941–1945', Japanese Monograph No. 26, Headquarters United States Army Japan, Office of the Military History Officer, Foreign Histories Division, 20 November 1957, Box 22 AL 5256.
Colonel Itsu Ogawa and Lieutenant-Colonel Ino Sei, 'Borneo Operations (Kawaguchi Detachment) 1941–1942', Japanese Studies in World War II, Box 6 AL 1099.

Public Record Office, Kew

'The Administration of the Occupied Territories in the Vital Southern Area', Special Intelligence Bulletin: Japanese Plans and Operation in S.E. Asia – Translation of Japanese Documents, 21 December 1945, W0 203/6310, Document 3.
'British Territories in North Borneo', extract from Allied Land Forces South-East Asia (A.L.F.S.E.A.), Wartime Intelligence Report (W.I.R.), No. 52, 28 September 1945, WO 208/105.
'Borneo: Oilfields, 19 September 1945, WO 208/104.
'First Division: Monthly Report for February, 1946', WO 203/5983.
'Guerilla Operations in British North Borneo', Report of Lim King Fatt, Chairman of the Administrative Board, Overseas Chinese Patriot Guerilla Band and Intelligence Officer of Guerilla Band, to Commanding Officer 125th Infantry Regiment, 10th Military District, 2 November 1943, WO 208/1053.
'"How I Happened to Come to Tawi Tawi" by Lim King Fatt, Chairman of the Administrative Board, Overseas Chinese Patriot Guerilla Band and Intelligence Officer of Guerilla Band, to Commanding Officer 125th Infantry Regiment, 10th Military District, 2 November 1943', WO 208/1053.
'Information Regarding Position in Nth. Borneo Obtained from Capt. Hamner, 14 April [19]44', WO 208/1053.
'Intelligence Bulletin No. 237, Item 2178: Interrogation of Manabu KUJI, Governor of West Coast (Jesselton) Province (20 Nov. 1943–1

Jun. 1945), North Borneo; Subject: Japanese Civil Administration in British North Borneo; c. mid-1946', WO 203/6317.

'Intelligence Bulletin No. 237, Item 2182: Interrogation of Lieutenants Yoshihiko WAKAMATSU and Kenzo MORIKAWA, and Captains Ryuji IKENO, Minoru TASUMA and Yoshio WATANABE, all officers attached to the North Borneo Volunteer Corps (KYODOTAI); Subject: North Borneo Volunteer Corps; c. mid-1946', WO 203/6317.

'Intelligence Bulletin No. 237, Item 2183: Interrogation of Lieutenant-General Masao BABA, General Officer Commanding 37th Army', WO 203/6317.

'Intelligence Bulletin No. 237, Item 2184: Interrogation of Major General Shigeru KURODA, 37th Army HQ; Subject: 12. Japanese Policy in Far East', WO 203/6317.

'Interrogation Report No. 21: Interrogation of Saburoo KAWADA, Senior Administrative Official in the Civil Administration, 4 Mar. 1946', WO 208/3114.

'Lieut. Kwok and Jesselton Area (from Capt. Hamner's Report)', WO 208/1053.

'Monthly Report for the Month of January, 1946', WO 203/5983.

'Monthly Report on Serian and Simunjan District by Capt. D.F.A.F.D. Morgan, Period from 15th February 1946 to 15th March 1946', WO 203/5983.

'Monthly Report for March 1946 for the Kuching District', WO 203/5983.

Order of battle including location, strength, disposition and movements of units and formations, Mar–Oct 1945 – Borneo, WO 208/1054.

'Orders Relating to the Occupation of the Vital Southern Area', Special Intelligence Bulletin: Japanese Plans and Operation in S.E. Asia – Translation of Japanese Documents, 21 December 1945, W0 203/6310, Document 2.

'Report No. 2 – Kuching', 6 October 1945, HQ Kuching Forces, 9 Australian Division AIF to Director of Naval Intelligence, Navy Office, Melbourne, WO 208/1054.

'Special Intelligence Bulletin: Japanese Plans and Operations in S.E. Asia – Translation of Japanese Documents, 21 Dec. 1945. Document 4: "Army-Navy-Central Agreement for establishing Military Administration in Occupied Territories"', WO 203/6310.

'Special Intelligence Bulletin: Japanese Plans and Operations in S.E. Asia – Translation of Japanese Documents, 21 Dec. 1945. Document 11: "Summary of the government of occupied territory in the Southern Area, 12 Oct. [19]42"', W0 203/6310.

'S.O.I. Legal to Liaison Officer, Kuching, 23 April 1946', WO 203/5991.

Rhodes House Library, Oxford

'Autobiography of C. F. C. Macaskie', Papers of C. F. C. Macaskie, MSS Pac. s. 71.

Boyd, T. Stirling. 'The Law and Constitution of Sarawak' (Typescript), 1934, MSS Pac. s. 86, Box 4 Item II.

Edward Brandah to Anthony Brooke, 26 October 1946, Brooke Papers, MSS Pac. s. 83, Box 13/1.

Joseph Law to Bertram Brooke, 31 May 1946, Brooke Papers, MSS Pac. s. 83, Box 2/3.

Noakes, J. L. 'Personal Report Upon My Experiences While Interned from 24th December 1941 to the 16th September 1945' (8 pp.) attached to 'Report Upon Defence Measures', MSS Pac. s. 62.

Noakes, J. L. 'Report Upon Defence Measures Adopted in Sarawak from June 1941 to the Occupation in December 1941 by Imperial Japanese Forces; also, an account of the movement of British and Sarawak Military Forces during the Japanese invasion of Sarawak', 15 February 1946, MSS Pac. s. 62.

'Statement by Mohd. Ma'amon bin Nor', 29 July 1946, Brooke Papers, MSS Pac. s. 83, Box 22.

Vyner Brooke to Bertram Brooke, May 1946, Brooke Papers, MSS Pac. s. 83, Box 19.

AUSTRALIAN WAR MEMORIAL ARCHIVES, CANBERRA

[British] Staff discussions with Netherlands East Indies at Singapore in 1940. Staff conversations with officers from NEI [Netherlands East Indies], Memorandum drawn up by Conference on operation between British and Dutch Forces in event of Japanese attack on Malaya, Borneo or Netherlands East Indies, 1941'. AWM54 213/1/3.

'British Staff conversation with Netherlands East Indies officers on co-operation in event of Japanese attack on Malaya, Borneo or Netherlands East Indies, 26–29: 1940'. AWM54 243/5/35.

'[Prisoners of War and Internees'] Report of investigations of the fate of Allied POW and Internees in British Borneo (namely British North Borneo, Labuan, Brunei and Sarawak). Compiled by Capt L. G. Darling, 9th Australian Division (August–December 1945)'. AWM54 779/1/25/

Sarawak Museum Archives, Kuching

'Annual Report of the District Officer, Kanowit, for the year 1946', Typescript.

Archer, J. B. 'Lintang Camp, Kuching, Sarawak. Official Documents and Papers Collected from the Records of the Civilian Internment Camp (No. 1 Camp) at Lintang, Kuching, Sarawak, during the years 1942–1943–1944–1945, Kuching', [1946?].

Order dated 14 May 1870, 'Orders which have not since been cancelled, issued by H.H. the Rajah of Sarawak or with his sanction from 1863 to 1890 inclusive', Kuching, 1891.

THESES AND OTHER UNPUBLISHED PAPERS

Cramb, R. A. 'The Impact of the Japanese Occupation on Agricultural Development in Sarawak', 1994/1995 MS (Personal Copy).

Lockard, C. A. 'The Southeast Asian Town in Historical Perspective: A Social History of Kuching, Malaysia, 1820–1970', 2 vols, PhD thesis, University of Wisconsin, 1973.

Ooi Keat Gin, 'Broken Promise?: Great Britain's Failure to Honour Treaty Obligations to Brooke Sarawak, a British Protectorate', 18th Annual Conference of the Association of Southeast Asian Studies in the United Kingdom (ASEASUK), School of Oriental and African Studies, University of London, London, U.K., 1–3 April 1998.

Ooi Keat Gin. 'Japanese Attitudes towards the Indigenous Peoples of Sarawak, 1914–1945', Symposium on the Japanese Occupation in South-East Asia, National University of Singapore, Singapore, 13–17 December 1995.

PUBLISHED OFFICIAL RECORDS

Annual Report on Sarawak for the Year 1947. Kuching: Government Printing Office, 1948.

Jones, L. W. Sarawak: *Report on the Census of Population taken on 15th June 1960*. Kuching: Government Printing Office, 1962.

Newman, C. L. *Report on Padi in Sarawak*. Kuching: Government Printing Office, 1938.

Noakes, J. L. *Sarawak and Brunei: A Report on the 1947 Population Census*. Kuching: Government Printing Office, 1950.

Sarawak Administration Report 1927. Kuching: Government Printing Office, 1928. Also, issued annually for the years 1928–38 inclusive.

Sarawak Information Service. *The Danger Within: A History of the Clandestine Communist Organization in Sarawak*. Kuching: Government Printing Office, 1963.

Seventh Malaysia Plan 1996–2000. Kuala Lumpur: Percetakan Nasional Malaysia. 1996.

SECONDARY SOURCES

Books

Adam-Smith, Patsy. *Prisoners of War: From Gallipoli to Korea*. Ringwood, Victoria: Viking/Penguin Books Australia, 1992.

Austin, *Ronald J. Let Enemies Beware! 'Caveant Hostes': The History of the 2/15th Battalion, 1940–1945*. McCrae: 2/15th Battalion AIF, Remembrance Club Inc., 1995.

Baring-Gould S. and C. A. Bampfylde. *A History of Sarawak under its Two White Rajahs, 1839–1908*. London: Henry Sotheran, 1909.

Benda, Harry J. *Continuity and Change in Southeast Asia*. Southeast Asia Studies No. 18, New Haven: Yale University Press, 1972.

Brooke, Anthony. *The Facts About Sarawak: A Documented Account of the Cession to Britain in 1946*. Bombay, 1947; reprinted Singapore: Summer Times, 1983.

Chin, John M. *The Sarawak Chinese*. Kuala Lumpur: Oxford University Press, 1981.

Crisswell, Colin N. *The End of the Brooke Raj in Sarawak*. Kiscadale Asia Research Series No. 1, Gartmore, Stirlingshire: Paul Strachan-Kiscadale, 1994.

Digby, K. H. *Lawyer in the Wilderness*. Cornell University Southeast Asia Program Data Paper No. 114, Ithaca, New York: Cornell University Press, October 1980.

Donnison, F. S. V. *British Military Administration in the Far East*. London: HMSO, 1956.

Donovan, Peter. *Waltzing Matildas: The Men and Machines of the 2/9th Australian Armoured Regimental Group in Australia and Borneo 1941–1946*. Blackwood, S. Australia: Donovan and Associates, 1988.

Edwards, Leonard, and Peter W. Stevens. *Short Histories of the Lawas and Kanowit Districts*. Kuching: Borneo Literature Bureau, 1971.

Elsbree, Willard. *Japan's Role in Southeast Asian Nationalist Movements 1940 to 1945*. New York: Institute of Pacific Relations, 1953.

Gill, G. Hermon. *Royal Australian Navy*. Canberra: Australian War Memorial, 1968.

Harrisson, Tom. *The Malays of South-West Sarawak Before Malaysia: A Socio-Ecological Survey*. London: Macmillan, 1970.

Harrisson, Tom. *World Within: A Borneo Story*. London: The Cresset Press, 1959.

Harvey-Ward, Ken. *The Sappers' War with Ninth Australian Division Engineers 1939–1945*. Neutral Bay, N.S.W.: Sakoga in conjunction with 9th Division RAE Association, 1992.

Horner, David. *The Gunners: A History of Australian Artillery*. St Leonards, N.S.W.: Allen and Unwin, 1995.

Howes, Peter H. H. *In a Fair Ground or Cibus Cassowarii*. London: Excalibur Press, 1994.

Jackson, James C. *Sarawak: A Geographical Survey of A Developing State*. London: University of London Press, 1968.

Jacob, Gertrude L. *The Raja of Sarawak: An Account of Sir James Brooke, K.C.B., LL.D., Given Chiefly Through Letters and Journals*. 2 vols, London: Macmillan, 1876.

Johnstone, Charlie. *To Sandakan: the diaries of Charlie Johnstone, prisoner of war 1942–45*. St Leonards, N.S.W.: Allen and Unwin, 1995.

Keith, Agnes Newton. *Three Came Home*. London: Michael Joseph, 1948.

Kirby, S. Woodburn, *et al. The War Against Japan Vol. I: The Loss of Singapore*. London: HMSO, 1957.

Lebra, Joyce C. *Japan's Greater East Asia Co-Prosperity Sphere in World War II: Selected Readings and Documents*. Kuala Lumpur: Oxford University Press, 1975.

Leigh, Michael B. *The Rising Moon: Political Change in Sarawak*. Sydney: Sydney University Press, 1974.

Liew Yung Tzu. *Sarawak Under the Japanese*. Sibu: Hua Ping Press, 1956 [text in Chinese].

Lockard, Craig Alan. *From Kampung to City: A Social History of Kuching, Malaysia, 1820–1970*. Ohio University Monographs in International Studies, Southeast Asia Series, No. 75, Athens, Ohio: Ohio University Press, 1987.

Long, Bob. *Operation Semut 1:'Z' Special Unit's Secret War; Soldiering with the Head-Hunters of Borneo*. Maryborough, Victoria: Australian Print Group, 1989.

Long, Gavin. *The Final Campaigns*. Canberra: Australian War Memorial, 1963.

Maxwell-Hall, J. *Kinabalu Guerillas: An Account of the Double Tenth 1943*. 2nd edn, Kuching: Sarawak Press, 1965.

Moffitt, Athol Randolph. *Project Kingfisher*. Sydney: Angus and Robertson, 1989.

Nelson, Hank. *P.O.W. Prisoners of War: Australians under Nippon*. Sydney: Australian Broadcasting Corporation, 1985.

Odgers, George. *Air War Against Japan*. Canberra: Australian War Memorial, 1957.

Ooi Keat Gin. *Of Free Trade and Native Interests: The Brookes and the Economic Development of Sarawak, 1841–1941*. Kuala Lumpur: Oxford University Press, 1997.

Ooi Keat Gin. *Japanese Empire in the Tropics: Selected Documents and Reports of the Japanese Period in Sarawak, Northwest Borneo, 1941–1945*. 2 vols, Ohio University Monographs, International Studies, South-East Asian Series, No. 101, Athens, Ohio: Ohio University Press, 1998.

Percival, A. E. *The War in Malaya*. London: Eyre & Spottiswoode, 1949.

Powell, Alan. *War by Stealth: Australians and the Allied Intelligence Bureau 1942–1945*. Melbourne: Melbourne University Press, 1996.

Purcell, Victor. *The Chinese in Malaya*. Kuala Lumpur: Oxford University Press, 1967.

Porritt, Vernom L. *British Colonial Rule in Sarawak 1946–1963*. Kuala Lumpur: Oxford University Press, 1997.

Reece, R. H. W. *The Name of Brooke: The End of White Rajah Rule in Sarawak*. Kuala Lumpur: Oxford University Press, 1982.

Robertson, Eric. *The Japanese File: Pre-War Japanese Penetration in Southeast Asia*. Singapore: Heinemann Asia, 1979.

Robertson, John. *Australia at War 1939–1945*. Melbourne: William Heinemann, 1981.

Runciman, Steven. *The White Rajahs: A History of Sarawak from 1841 to 1946*. Cambridge: Cambridge University Press, 1960.

Sanib Said. *Malay Politics in Sarawak 1946–1966: The Search for Unity and Political Ascendancy*. Singapore: Oxford University Press, 1985.

Shargava, K. D. and K. N. V. Sastri. *Official History of the Indian Armed Forces in the Second World War, 1939–45: Campaigns in South-East Asia, 1941–42*. Combined Inter-Services Historical Section India and Pakistan, City Orient Longmans, 1960.

Sutlive, Vinson H., Jr. *Tun Jugah of Sarawak: Colonialism and Iban Response*. Kuala Lumpur: Penerbit Fajar Bakti for Sarawak Literary Society, 1992.

T'ien Ju-K'ang. *The Chinese of Sarawak: A Study of Social Structure*. Monograph on Social Anthropology No. 12, London: Department of Anthropology, London School of Economics and Political Science, 1953.

Trebeck, Bruce, et al. (ed.). *'What We Have ... We Hold!' A History of the 2/17 Australian Infantry Battalion 1940–1945*. Balgowlah, N.S.W.: 2/17 Battalion History Committee, 1998.

Tregonning, K. G. *A History of Modern Sabah (North Borneo 1881–1963)*. 2nd ed. Singapore: University of Malaya Press, 1965.

Wall, Don. *Kill the Prisoners*. Sydney: D. Wall, 1996.

Wigmore, Lionel. *The Japanese Thrust*. Canberra: Australian War Memorial, 1957.

Wong Kim Min, James (ed.). *'No Joke, James': The World according to William Wong Tsap En*. Singapore: Summer Times Publishing, 1985.

Articles

Akashi, Yoji. 'The Japanese Occupation of Malaya: Interruption or Transformation?', in *Southeast Asia Under Japanese Occupation*, ed. Alfred W. McCoy, Monograph Series No. 22, Yale University Southeast Asia Studies, New Haven: Yale University Press, 1980, pp. 65–90.

Anderson, Benedict R. O'G. 'Japan: "The Light of Asia"', in *Southeast Asia in World War II: Four Essays*, ed. Josef Silverstein, Southeast Asia Studies No. 7, New Haven: Yale University Press, 1966, pp. 13–50.

Batson, Benjamin A. 'Siam and Japan: The Perils of Independence', in *Southeast Asia Under Japanese Occupation*, ed., Alfred W. McCoy, Monograph Series No. 22, Yale University Southeast Asia Studies, New Haven: Yale University Press, 1980, pp. 267–302.

Cheah Boon Kheng. 'The Social Impact of the Japanese Occupation on Malaya (1942–1945)', in *Southeast Asia Under Japanese Occupation*, ed. Alfred W. McCoy, Monograph Series No. 22, Yale University Southeast Asia Studies, New Haven: Yale University Press, 1980, pp. 91–124.

Chong Ah Onn, '1943–46, Fifth Division, Sarawak', Part I *SG*, 29 November 1952, pp. 263–5; Part II *SG*, 31 December 1952, pp. 283–7; and Part III *SG*, 30 January 1953, pp. 11–13.

Francis, Simon. 'Wartime Intelligence Reports on Borneo', *BRB*, 25 (1993) 137–41.

Guyot, Dorothy. 'Burma Independence Army: A Political Movement in Military Garb', in *Southeast Asia in World War II: Four Essays*, ed. Josef Silverstein, New Haven: Yale University, Southeast Asia Studies No. 7, 1966, pp. 51–65.

Harrisson, Tom. 'The Chinese in Borneo 1942–1946', *IA*, 26, 3 (July 1950) 354–62.

Hipkins, James R. 'The History of the Chinese in Borneo', *SMJ*, 19, 38–9 (July-December 1971) 125–46.

Horton, A. V. M. 'A Note on the British Retreat from Kuching, 1941–1942', *SMJ*, 36, 57 (December 1986) 241–9.

Howes, Peter H. H. 'The Lintang Camp: Reminiscences of an internee during the Japanese Occupation, 1942–1945', *JMHSSB*, 2 (March 1976) 33–47.

Huggett, C. 'The Borneo Campaign', in *Bayonets Abroad: A History of the 2/13 Battalion A.I.F. in the Second World War*, ed. G. H. Fearnside, Swanbourne, W. Australia: John Burridge, 1993, pp. 383–406.

'The Japanese Occupation: Extracts from a broadcast interview with Tan Sri Ong Kee Hui by Christopher Chan on 14 February 1975', *JMHSSB*, 3 (December 1976) 4–14.

Kroef, Justus M. Van Der. 'Communism and Chinese Communalism in Sarawak', *CQ*, 20 (October–December 1964) 38–66.

Kroef, Justus M. Van Der. 'Communism in Sarawak Today', *AS*, 6, 10 (October 1956) 568–79.

Lockard, Craig A. 'Leadership and Power Within the Chinese Community of Sarawak: An Historical Survey', *JSEAS*, 2, 2 (September 1971) 195–217.

Lockard, Craig A. 'The 1857 Chinese Rebellion in Sarawak: A Reappraisal', *JSEAS*, 9, 1 (March 1978) 85–98.

Marr, David G. 'World War II and the Vietnamese Revolution', in *Southeast Asia under Japanese Occupation*, ed. Alfred W. McCoy, Southeast Asia Studies No. 22, New Haven: Yale University, 1980, pp. 125–58.

McCoy, Alfred W. '"Politics By Other Means": World War II in the Western Visayas, Philippines', in *Southeast Asia under Japanese Occupation*, ed. Alfred W. McCoy, Southeast Asia Studies No. 22, New Haven: Yale University, 1980, pp. 191–245.

Morrison, Ian. 'Local Self-Government in Sarawak', *PA*, 22, 2 (June 1949) 178–85.

Ooi Keat Gin. 'Chinese Vernacular Education in Sarawak During Brooke Rule, 1841–1946', *MAS*, 28, 3 (July 1994) 503–31.

Ooi Keat Gin. 'For Want of Rice: Sarawak's Attempts at Rice Self-Sufficiency During the Period of Brooke Rule, 1841–1941', *JSEAS* 29, 1(March 1998) 8–23.

Ooi Keat Gin. 'Education in Sarawak During the Period of Colonial Administration, 1946–1963', *JMBRAS*, 63, 2 (December 1990) 35–68.

Ooi Keat Gin. 'Mission Education in Sarawak During the Period of Brooke Rule, 1841–1946', *SMJ*, 62, 63 (December 1991) 283–373.

Ooi Keat Gin. 'Sarawak Malay Attitudes Towards Education During the Brooke Period, 1841–1946', *JSEAS*, 21, 2 (September 1990) 340–59.

Pole-Evans, R. J. 'The Supreme Council, Sarawak', *SMJ*, 7, 7 (June 1956) 98–108.

Pringle, Robert. 'Asun's "Rebellion": The Political Growing Pains of a Tribal Society in Brooke Sarawak, 1929–1940', *SMJ*, 16, 32–3 (July-December 1968) 346–76.

Purden, Ivor M. 'Japanese P.O.W. Camps in Borneo', in *Borneo: The Japanese P.O.W. Camps – Mail of the Forces, P.O.W. and Internees*, Neville Watterson, Wellingborough: W. N. Watterson, 1989, pp. 20–24.

Saunders, Graham. 'The Bau Chinese Attack on Kuching, February 1857: A Different Perspective', *SMJ*, 42, 63 (December 1991) 375–96.

Stanley, Peter. '"Sniffing the ground": Australians and Borneo – 1945, 1994', *JAWM*, 25 (October 1994) 32, 37–43.

Steinberg, David. 'The Philippine "Collaborators": Survival of an Oligarchy', in *Southeast Asia in World War II: Four Essays*, ed. Josef Silverstein, Southeast Asia Studies No. 7, New Haven: Yale University, 1966, pp. 67–86.

Taylor, Robert H. 'Burma in the Anti Fascist War', in *Southeast Asia under Japanese Occupation*, ed. Alfred W. McCoy, Southeast Asia Studies No. 22, New Haven: Yale University, 1980, pp. 159–90.

Waters. Gary. 'The Labuan Island and Brunei Bay Operation', in *Australian Army Amphibious Operations in the South-West Pacific: 1942–45*, ed. Gleen Wahlert, Papers of the Australian Army History Conference held at the Australian War Memorial, 15 November 1994, Canberra: Australian Army Doctrine Centre, 1995, pp. 71–102.

Index

Abdillah, *Datu Patinggi* Abang Haji, 70

Abdul Rahman, Haji: 'a noted intellectual and religious scholar', 45; appointed *ken-sanji* (councillor), 45

Adat (native), 3

Adenan, Acting District Officer, 47

'Administration Report for 1934', 10

'Administration of the Occupied Territories in the Vital Southern Area' (25 November 1941), 39–40

Aerial reconnaissance (Allied), 51

Agricultural Training Centre, Tarat (f 1942), 52

Agricultural stations, 52–3, 65 (n 48)

Agriculture, 71; *see also* Food, Rice, Poultry, Rubber, Vegetables

Air Raid Precautions (ARP), 49

Air raids: by the Allies, 51–2, 57, 70, 73, 125, 126, 128; by the Japanese, 34, 39, 61 (n 1), 125

Anti-aircraft guns, 30

Antimony, 5

Archer, J. Beville, 36, 37 (n 15), 68 (n 76), 125

Arden-Clarke, Sir Charles Noble, 93

Area Headmen (Chinese), 102

Asia for Asians (concept), 55, 60

Assistant District Officers, 3

Asun, *Penghulu*, 15 (n 6)

Australia: Europeans flee to, 33, 79

Australian military units: 7th Division, 89; 8th Division, 110 (n 6); 9th Division, 89–92, 97, 108 (n 2); 29th Motor Transport Royal Australian Service Corps, 110 (n 6); Royal Australian Air Force, 92

Australians, 58, 122

Bailey, C. W., 27

Bajaus, 48

Balikpapan, 25, 89

Banggi Island, 20

Baram, 31: Iban killings of Chinese (1945) at, 97, 99; location of, 2; SRD recruits in, 100

Barisan Pemuda Sarawak (Sarawak Youth Front), 96

Batang Lupar, *see* Lupar River

Bates, Miss H. E., 111 (n 7)

Batu Lintang Internment Camp, 33, 36, 39, 58, 79–84, 84–5, 88 (n 38), 128; categories of internee at, 58; danger of keeping of a diary in, 88 (n 38); fencing at, 59; forced labour at, 57, 60; guards at, 59; ill-health in, 80; Japanese contingency plan for the elimination of prisoners at, 110–11 (n 7); prisoners of war 'treated more severely than civilian internees' at, 59–60; RAAF drops relief supplies at, 92; rules and regulations at, 59; starvation in, 83–4; survivors, 84, 92, 121–2, 129

Deputy Secretary for Defence,
Sarawak [Elam, H. Edgar
H.], 38 (n 17)
Digby, K. H., 68 (n 76)
Direction Finding Station (DFS),
Kuching, 35
District Officers, 3, 6
Double Tenth Revolt (1943),
56–7, 61 (n 4), 62 (n 5), 65
(n 38), 117
Dusuns, 48
Dutch: military activity, 62–3
(n 6); nationals (held in Batu
Lintang Camp), 58
Dutch Borneo, 30, 89, 97, 99
Dutch East Indies, 22; long-term
significance of Japanese
interregnum in, 123; oil
supplier to Japan, 23

Eastick, Brigadier Thomas C.,
90–1, 92, 128
Education, 15 (n 7–8), 87 (n 21),
129–30; Chinese, 43, 104,
106–7; indigenous, 15 (n 8);
Malay, 6, 15 (n 7), 43;
see also Illiteracy
Elsbree, Willard, 123
Europeans, 4, 13–14, 69;
'arrogance verging on
stupidity' of, 80; in the
Brooke civil service, 112
(n 19); discouragement of
investment by, 13–14; flee
from Sarawak, 33–4; held in
Batu Lintang Camp, 58;
Japanese treatment of, 39,
42, 58–60, 79–84; number of,
4; *see also* Batu Lintang
Internment Camp

Fifth Division (Sarawak), 109 (n 3)
Firearms, 71–2, 118
First Division (Sarawak): Chinese
migration in, 57; Chinese
political activity in, 105–6;
Japanese census of, 50

Fishing, 67 (n 73), 71
Foochow (dialect group), 114
(n 39); and the SCA, 120
Food: production, 42, 51–4, 118,
129; rationing, 128, 129;
shortages, 70, 83, 118, 129;
supplies, 77–8, 79–80;
see also Rice
Formosa, 20
Formosans, 59
Fourth Division (Sarawak), 109
(n 3)
French Indo-China, 22
Fruit, 77
Fujino force, 109 (n 5)
Fund-raising: for the Japanese
war effort, 43; *see also*
Chinese, Taxation

Gading, 129
'Ginnie' (a secret generator),
82–3
Gold, 43
Gold-mining, 9, 129
Grave-robbing, 83
Great Britain, *see* United
Kingdom
Greater East Asia Co-Prosperity
Sphere, 22, 23, 55, 60, 74
Grey, Lord (third Earl Grey,
1802–94), 15 (n 5)
Guan Soon (Lawas), 54, 78
Guarantee system (*re*
immigrants), 10
Guncho (District Officer), 46, 75
Gunseibu Government (Japanese
military administration in
north-west Borneo), 39–68,
71, 76; 'decentralized and
participatory', 43;
'dominated by military
personnel', 40; general
policies of, 40–4; 'good
relations' with the
indigenous population (until
latter half of 1944), 70; loss
of civil affairs staff, 40;